JEREMY THORPE

A DAZZLINGLY TALENTED MAN

PHILIP DALLING

HALSGROVE

First published in Great Britain in 2018

British Library Cataloguing-in-Publication Data
A CIP record for this title is available from the British Library

ISBN 978 0 85704 336 8

HALSGROVE
Halsgrove House,
Ryelands Business Park,
Bagley Road, Wellington, Somerset TA21 9PZ
Tel: 01823 653777 Fax: 01823 216796
email: sales@halsgrove.com

Part of the Halsgrove group of companies
Information on all Halsgrove titles is available at: www.halsgrove.com

Printed and bound by Parksons Graphics, India

What They Said About Jeremy Thorpe

"Thorpe, certainly to those of us whose public awareness came of age in the mid-1960s, had more wit and charm than a whole planeload of Tony Blairs".
Journalist David Randall, writing in the *Independent on Sunday* in 2009.

"Jeremy Thorpe's leadership and resolve were the driving force that continued the Liberal revival that began under Jo Grimond."
Sir Nick Clegg, Deputy Prime Minister of the United Kingdom from 2010 to 2015 and Leader of the Liberal Democrats from 2007 to 2015.

"The infamy of Jeremy Thorpe's downfall unfairly colours all else in his life. Thorpe was a stylish, progressive and popular politician. Under his leadership the Liberal Party won more votes than ever before or since at a general election and helped drive legislation taking Britain into the European Community through a divided Parliament. But the much-promised breakthrough never came and Thorpe's reluctant resignation left the Liberal Party in a state from which many predicted it would be unable to recover."
Julian Glover writing on the *Liberal History website.*

"He had a genuine sympathy for the underprivileged - whether in his beloved North Devon where his first campaign was for 'mains, drains and a little bit of light' or in Africa, where he was a resolute fighter against apartheid."
Lord Steel of Aikwood, who succeeded Jeremy Thorpe as leader of the Liberal Party.

"Thorpe's Liberalism was essentially romantic and emotional. He reacted strongly against bone-headed Establishment snobbery, arrogant management or racial injustice, but showed scant interest in formulating any coherent political philosophy. On the other hand there was no doubting Thorpe's quick mind or his keen antennae. He was to the fore in predicting the 1967 devaluation crisis and in identifying the mounting crisis in Ulster; he also showed himself a consistent supporter of Britain's entry into the Common Market."
Anonymous obituary in the *Daily Telegraph*.

"Jeremy Thorpe was a colossal figure in the revival of the Liberal cause in post-war Britain. In North Devon he was a greatly loved champion of the community and is remembered with huge affection to this day."
Sir Nick Harvey, former Liberal Democrat minister and Member of Parliament for North Devon.

"In Barnstaple, Mr Jeremy Thorpe's constituency, all anyone ever talks about is Jeremy. 'Jeremy is the Liberal Party', one party worker told me.'We want your support for Jeremy'is what canvassers say on the doorstep."
Caroline Moorehead writing in *The Times* before the February 1974 General Election.

"Jeremy Thorpe was without equal as a constituency member":
Tony Speller, Conservative PM for North Devon 1979-1992, speaking after his victory over Thorpe in the 1979 General Election.

"Jeremy Thorpe was the best MP North Devon ever had or ever will have"
Raymond Liverton, Honorary Alderman of North Devon, former Independent councillor and, in his personal politics, a lifelong Conservative.

"He had an extraordinary ability both to cheer up his followers and send up his opponents."
The journalist **Christopher Booker**

Contents

Acknowledgements

Credit for the original idea for this book belongs to Steven Pugsley, chairman of the Halsgrove Group. It has been made possible through the co-operation of people who were politically active during the Jeremy Thorpe years.

Special thanks are due to Malcolm Prowse, whose parents Jack and Lilian saved North Devon Liberals from virtual extinction. Malcolm, his sisters Margaret and Liz (Spear), their brother Richard and Liz's husband Derrick shared the triumphs and disasters of Jeremy Thorpe's political life. I am grateful not just for the information and insights they provided, but also for their constant encouragement.

Peter Bray was Lilian Prowse's assistant agent in North Devon for many of the Thorpe years, succeeded her as agent, and built a legendary reputation as the architect of Liberal, Liberal/SDP Alliance and Liberal Democrat by-election victories. He has been generous with his time and memories and also encouraged the project at every step.

A major role in Liberal successes in North Devon during the Thorpe era was played by the Young Liberals, who in this constituency at least were more interested in getting their candidate elected than in political posturing. David Worde, a respected local councillor, led the Young Liberals in North Devon and I am grateful for his help.

Thanks also to Sir Nick Harvey who won back North Devon for the Liberals and represented the constituency for an unprecedented 23 years, achieving ministerial office in the Coalition Government of 2010-2015. I also have to thank Chris Mullin, who contested North Devon for Labour in 1970 and later achieved ministerial rank as MP for Sunderland South, for permission to quote extensively from his memoir, *Hinterland*.

My fellow journalists at the *North Devon Gazette*, former editor Andy Keeble and Tony Gussin were very helpful. Many more people, of all political colours, consented to talk to me, on or off the record. It would be impossible to name them all individually but I must mention Marcus and Denzil Bath, Professor John Beckett, Albert Cook, Roger and Anne Dapling, Tony Freeman, Raymond Liverton, Sir Richard Peek, Alec Pickersgill and Gerald Waldon.

Last, but certainly not least, my grateful thanks to Brenda Dyer for her invaluable assistance with my research, for her ideas and, above all, for her unflagging support.

Author's Note

The author's hope is that the story of a remarkable man whose name still resonates across North Devon and the United Kingdom as a whole will appeal to the general reader as well as to political aficionados. For that reason the first chapter of this book attempts to explain the colourful but complex history of radical politics in the West Country, set against the wider context of the national political scene as it was in the late nineteenth century and throughout the twentieth century.

The story continues with a review of Jeremy Thorpe's early life, his family background and the influences which helped to shape him, continuing into his schooldays and his time at Oxford University, possibly the most crucial period of his political development. It moves on to examine the factors that brought him to North Devon and reviews his years as a Member of Parliament, leader of the Liberal party, and a statesman of considerable repute in the wider world, particularly in those African and other developing nations whose cause he championed to great effect.

The second part of the book looks at Thorpe through the eyes of the several categories of people who promoted or closely followed his career – the professionals, the party activists, the voters and, tellingly for a man respected and admired by many of those whose opinions were far removed from his own, his political opponents.

The principal theme of the book is the positive contribution made by Jeremy Thorpe to life in Britain, and particularly to his constituency of North Devon, during years of considerable political upheaval. The work would nevertheless lack credibility if it attempted to ignore the events of the 1970s, which brought Thorpe to the dock of the Old Bailey to face perhaps the most serious charges ever to be made against a politician in the modern age.

The story ends with Thorpe's twilight years, which brought belated honours from the Liberal party both nationally and locally and, in the author's opinion, at least a partial recognition that the tragi-comedy of what has become known as the Scott Affair was a wholly inadequate way of recognising what in many ways was a remarkable political career.

For the statistically minded the appendices tell the story of Jeremy Thorpe's political campaigns, and celebrate the memory of remarkable family political dynasties closely associated with the Liberal Party and the West Country. The third appendix recalls the Liberal by-election triumph of 1958 in the Torrington constituency which preceded, and in many ways heralded, Thorpe's own 1959 breakthrough.

The history of the Liberal party itself is complicated, with a number of splits occurring over the 159 years since the party was founded in May 1859. The following paragraphs hopefully act as a brief guide to the different groups which at various times included the word 'Liberal' in their titles.

The Liberal party was born as a result of a merger between three political groupings, the Whigs, the Radicals and the Peelites (a breakaway faction from the Conservative party which supported the former Prime Minister and Conservative Leader Sir Robert Peel). In 1988 the Liberal party become the Liberal Democrats, as a result of a merger with the Social Democratic party, a splinter group from the Labour party. From 1981 until the merger the two groups had formed the SDP-Liberal Alliance for electoral purposes.

The Liberal Unionist party was formed in 1886 by a faction that broke away from the Liberal party, forming a political alliance with the Conservatives in opposition to Irish Home Rule. The Liberal Unionists and the Conservatives ruled in a coalition Unionist government from 1895 to 1905, retaining separate organisations until a full merger in 1912.

The National Liberal party (known until 1948 as the Liberal National party), was a liberal political party in the United Kingdom from 1931 to 1968. The Liberal Nationals evolved as a distinctive group within the Liberal party over the issues initially arising from the official party's support for the minority Labour government led by Ramsay MacDonald and later from MacDonald's 1931 National Government. The Liberal Nationals later co-operated with and eventually merged with the Conservative party.

Conservative and Unionist is the formal name of the Conservative party in the UK and over the years many Conservative MPs sat as Conservative and Unionist or simply as Unionists. The term signifies support for the Union of England, Wales, Scotland and Northern Ireland.

Philip Dalling
Chittlehampton
North Devon 2018

Introduction

Given the heady mix of drama and tragedy, allied to the undoubted glamour and appeal of the man himself, it seems completely apt to use theatrical metaphors to describe the impact of Jeremy Thorpe upon the people of Great Britain and, in particular of North Devon, the Parliamentary constituency he first nursed and then represented for almost three decades.

If Thorpe had the necessary star quality to draw and hold an audience, he was fortunate in having the backing of a first rate supporting cast, headed by a superb producer/director in the shape of his loyal, long-serving and ultra-professional agent, Lilian Prowse, with her sharp political instincts and unrivalled knowledge of the stage which was the North Devon constituency.

Her talents were ably supported by her young assistant agent Peter Bray, who was to become a legend in his own lifetime in Liberal Party circles as a wandering magician, waving his wand over moribund local parties from the suburban home counties to the English/Scottish borders, when those parties suddenly found themselves on the brink of winnable by-elections.

Lilian Prowse's political Oscar-winning masterpiece was her role in delivering Thorpe's massive 11,000 vote majority in the February 1974 General Election. Peter Bray's great triumph was achieved in the unlikely territory of Bermondsey in south-east London, a safe Labour seat until Bray conjured up a 44 per cent swing to the Liberals.

Thorpe as the star vehicle and Prowse and Bray as the architects of electoral success captured the headlines. Behind them, in the market towns, villages, hamlets and farmsteads of North Devon, in the Taw Valley (and for a spell along the Torridge too), and in the remote fastnesses of Exmoor, were the Liberal councillors, political activists and the foot-soldier party members who raised funds, argued and canvassed to an extent never experienced in the constituency either before or since.

It was politics on an apparently homely and simple scale, yet carefully thought out and enthusiastically executed. Its importance in a wider context lies in the belief that it was the foundation of what became known as community politics. The techniques were used to great advantage nationally during the Liberal revival which reached its apogee in 2005, when the party, reduced in the 1950s to five MPs, returned 62 MPs to the House of Commons. Community politics were forged on the streets and in the lanes of North Devon.

Jeremy Thorpe always claimed to have laid the foundation for a Liberal revival, which came to fruition during his lifetime in the shape of a steadily increasing, if still modest parliamentary representation. Thorpe lived long enough to see the Liberals' re-acquaintance with the corridors of power in 2010 when, despite winning five fewer seats than at the previous General Election, the party under Nick Clegg held the balance of power and entered into a formal coalition government with David Cameron's Conservatives, ending thirteen years of Labour rule under Tony Blair and Gordon Brown.

Thorpe himself had come relatively close to holding the balance of power after the February 1974 hung General Election, when the outgoing Conservative leader Edward Heath attempted to cling on to power by reaching some sort of arrangement with the now 14-strong Liberals – 8 more than were elected in 1970. Jeremy himself could have expected high office under such an arrangement, with the posts of Home Secretary and Foreign Secretary, both high offices of state, mentioned.

Although sections of the press at the time worked themselves into a lather of speculation, a workable agreement was always unlikely. Even with Liberal support, Heath was well short of a majority, and would have been dependent (shades of Theresa May post-2017) upon MPs from Northern Ireland, who in the troubled 1970s were much more volatile and less united as a group than today.

The second 1974 General Election in the autumn of that year gave Harold Wilson a small majority. By the time Wilson had quit the political scene and Labour's majority under his successor Jim Callaghan had dwindled away, leading to the Lib-Lab alliance (not a formal coalition) Jeremy Thorpe had resigned as Liberal leader (in May 1976).

In the years to follow the emphasis shifted from his undoubted political abilities to the allegations that led to his appearance at the Old Bailey in 1979, accused of incitement to murder and conspiracy to murder.

Although being acquitted, his reputation was badly damaged and he was never again to play any substantial part in public life. His diagnosis with Parkinson's Disease in 1981, when he was only in his early fifties, ensured that there was to be no comeback. Thorpe had never held any office of state during his twenty-year Westminster career, although he was appointed to the Privy Council. It was his eventual successor as MP for North Devon Nick (now Sir Nicholas) Harvey who was to hold ministerial office under the 2010-2015 Conservative/Liberal coalition government.

In later years the Liberals and Liberal Democrats, both nationally and in North Devon, provided Thorpe with some consolation for his shattered career by acknowledging his contribution to politics, locally, nationally, and on the world stage. Yet even in defeat, and with his reputation badly damaged by the revelations which emerged during what has become known as the Norman Scott affair, Jeremy Thorpe continued to command centre stage.

It was very aptly summed up in the wake of the 1979 General Election. His victorious Conservative opponent Tony Speller, hit the nail on the head when he lamented, apropos of his overwhelming poll victory in North Devon:

'Everyone knows who lost, but no one remembers yet who won'.

Jeremy Thorpe Timeline

Personal Life	Political Background
1929. John Jeremy Thorpe born South Kensington, 29 April, son of John Henry Thorpe and Ursula, née Norton Griffiths.	**1929.** Labour minority government elected 30 May. Prime Minister James Ramsay MacDonald, Leader of Opposition Stanley Baldwin (Con), Liberal leader David Lloyd George.
1939. With war looming Thorpe family move to Limpsfield, Surrey. Jeremy evacuated to the United States, where he attends Rectory School in Connecticut from September.	**1939.** 3 September Chamberlain announces that Great Britain is at war with Germany, after Hitler invades Poland.
1943. Jeremy Thorpe returns to England aboard Royal Navy cruiser HMS *Phoebe*. Starts school at Eton College.	**1943.** Winston Churchill leading wartime coalition government at Westminster.
1947. Thorpe leaves Eton. National Service curtailed after six weeks. Works as preparatory schoolmaster.	**1947.** First majority Labour government led by Clement Attlee in office after winning landslide victory over Churchill's Conservatives in 1945. Clement Davies succeeds Sir Archibald Sinclair as leader of the Liberal party.
1948. October Jeremy Thorpe goes up to Trinity College, Oxford to read law.	**1948.** National Health Service launched by Health Minister Aneurin Bevan on 5 July.
1949. November. Thorpe becomes President of Oxford University Liberal Club.	**1949.** April 4. Great Britain signs the North Atlantic Treaty, creating NATO.
1950. April, Thorpe's 21st birthday. Applies to be placed on list of Liberal Parliamentary candidates.	**1950.** Attlee's Labour Party wins General Election with majority of five seats. Clement Davies leads Liberals with 9 MPs, three fewer than at 1945 election.
1951. Thorpe is President of the Oxford Union for Hilary Term of 1951.	**1951.** Attlee calls second General Election. Churchill and Conservatives return to power. Liberals under Davies reduced to 6 seats.
1952. Jeremy Thorpe completes law studies and is adopted as Liberal candidate for North Devon.	**1952.** Prime Minister Churchill announces that Britain has an atomic bomb.
1954. February. Jeremy Thorpe called to the bar and also works as a television journalist.	**1954.** Strike in autumn cripples London docks.

1955. Thorpe contests first General Election substantially cutting Tory majority in North Devon.

1955. Churchill's successor Anthony Eden Eden wins General Election, with majority of 60. Liberals, remain static at six seats.

1957. North Devon Liberals publish booklet to celebrate five years of Thorpe as candidate.

1957. Liberals, now led by Jo Grimond, have just five MPs after losing a by-election.

1958. Thorpe campaigns in Torrington and helps Mark Bonham Carter win by-election.

1958. The European Economic Community (EEC) comes into being.

1959. Jeremy Thorpe wins North Devon at General Election and makes maiden speech in Parliament.

1959. Third consecutive Conservative victory led by Harold Macmillan. Liberals only gain is in North Devon.

1961. Thorpe forms Winnable Seats project to focus resources on constituencies that Liberals have good chance of gaining.

1961. UK application for EEC membership vetoed by French President Charles de Gaulle.

1962. Winnable Seats idea pays dividend as Liberals win Orpington by-election.

1962. Britain and France agree to develop Concorde supersonic airliner.

1964. Thorpe increases his majority to more than 5,000 votes in October General Election.

1964. Labour's Harold Wilson has majority of just four seats. Liberals up to nine seats.

1966. Thorpe majority at General Election cut drastically by new Tory contender Tim Keigwin.

1966. Labour majority soars to 96. Liberal revival continues with 12 seats secured.

1967. January. Jeremy Thorpe succeeds Jo Grimond as leader of the Liberal party.

1967. Prime Minister Harold Wilson announces that the UK will apply again for EEC membership.

1968. May. Thorpe marries Caroline Allpass. The couple are on their honeymoon when Liberal plotters launch unsuccessful bid to depose him as leader.

1968. Following the 'Honeymoon Plot' Liberal Party executive backs Thorpe by 48 votes to 2.

1969. Jeremy and Caroline Thorpe's son Rupert born in April.

1969. By-election boost as Liberals win Birmingham Ladywood from Labour.

1970. Election fright for Thorpe as Tory Tim Keigwin cuts majority to 369. Sadness as Caroline Thorpe dies in car crash.

1970. Edward Heath's Tories topple Wilson and Labour. Liberal revival stalled as MPs halved to six.

1972. Caroline Thorpe monument dedicated on Codden Hill in North Devon constituency.

1972. Electoral success for Liberals with Victory in the Rochdale by-election.

1973. March. Jeremy Thorpe marries concert pianist Marion Stein.

1973. Major electoral successes for Liberals as the party wins four seats at by-elections.

1974. February. First of two General Elections in year sees Jeremy Thorpe's greatest electoral triumph recording 11,082 majority.

1974. February. Thorpe-led Liberals win 14 seats and record six million votes. Talks with Edward Heath about a coalition come to nothing.

1974. October. Liberal majority in North Devon is reduced by new Tory contender Tony Speller. Norman Scott allegations continue to cause problems for Thorpe.

1974. October. Wilson wins narrow majority. Liberal disappointment as party wins one seat less than at February poll.

1975. October. Andrew Newton makes a bungled attempt to shoot Norman Scott on Exmoor. Newton shoots Scott's dog, Rinka.

1975. February. Margaret Thatcher defeats Edward Heath in Conservative leadership election.

1976. January. Department for Trade publishes report into collapse of London and County Securities. Thorpe is criticised for failure to investigate the true nature of the company. In May Thorpe resigns as Liberal leader and is replaced by David Steel.

1976. March. Former leader Jo Grimond claims Liberal party's poor results in by-elections is due to a lack of confidence in Jeremy Thorpe caused by increasing media coverage of the Scott affair.

1977. Media interest in the Scott affair intensifies and increases pressure on Jeremy Thorpe.

1977. Liberal leader David Steel and new Prime Minister Jim Callaghan agree Lib-Lab pact.

1978. Thorpe's last speech in House of Commons. He remains MP for North Devon but withdraws from public life. In August he is charged with conspiracy and incitement to murder.

1978. May. David Steel announces end of the Lib-Lab pact. Labour is again a minority government.

1979. Thorpe accepts invitation to fight North Devon at General Election in May. His Old Bailey trial postponed until after the election. Thorpe loses to Tory Tony Speller.

1979. Callaghan's minority government loses a vote of confidence. In General Election Margaret Thatcher's Conservatives win majority of 43. Liberals lose two seats.

1979. The trial of Thorpe and co-defendants begins in May and lasts six weeks. Jury acquits Thorpe and others on all charges. Thorpe's Parkinson's Disease is first diagnosed.

1979. Jeremy Thorpe accepts that there is now no role for him in the Liberal party and announces he will not again seek to contest an election.

1982. Thorpe's appointment as Director of the British section of Amnesty International is opposed by much of the membership and he withdraws from the post.

1982. June 14. The Falklands War ends as British forces re-occupy Port Stanley.

1983. Conservative Tony Speller holds North Devon at June General Election

1983. Margaret Thatcher, riding on a tide of popularity following the re-capture of the

Election against Thorpe's successor as Liberal candidate, Roger Blackmore.

1987. At the June General Election Tory MP Speller wins North Devon for third time. Jeremy Thorpe appointed President of local Liberals.

1992. Nick Harvey regains North Devon for the Liberal Democrats, defeating Tony Speller.

1997. Jeremy Thorpe receives standing ovation at Lib Dem conference. Harvey retains North Devon with 6,000 majority.

2009. Jeremy Thorpe's final public appearance to unveil bust of himself in the Grimond Room at Westminster.

2010. Nick Harvey wins fifth General Election in North Devon and is given ministerial post in new coalition government.

2014. Marion Thorpe dies on 6 March, followed by the death of Jeremy Thorpe on 4 December. Nick Harvey pays tribute to Thorpe at the funeral on 17 December.

Falklands, wins a majority of 144. Liberals perform well and win total of 23 seats.

1987. Thatcher wins her third General Election against Labour's Neil Kinnock. Liberal/Social Democrat Alliance wins 23 seats.

1992. Conservatives win a fourth successive General Election under John Major. Lib Dems under Paddy Ashdown win 20 seats.

1997. Stunning election victory for Labour's Tony Blair. Lib Dems the other victors, with 28 gains taking total of seats in House to 46.

2009. In local elections the Liberal Democrats leapfrog Labour into second place behind the Conservatives, winning 28 per cent of the vote.

2010. David Cameron's Conservatives fall short of overall majority and enter into coalition with the Liberal Democrats.

2014. In the European Parliament election the United Kingdom Independence Party UKIP emerges ahead of Labour and the Conservatives, with a 27 per cent share of the votes cast.

PART ONE
Jeremy Thorpe and the Liberal Cause

To understand the reasons behind Jeremy Thorpe's passionate attachment to the ideals of both liberalism as a concept and the Liberals as a British political party, it is necessary to delve into the history of both the creed and the organisation which adopted its beliefs. It is particularly important, given that Thorpe's power base during his Parliamentary career was in North Devon, to examine the great appeal of liberalism, in the abstract and in terms of a political grouping, in the West Country, where it often marched side by side with the area's dominant nonconformist religion.

The first part of this book surveys radical politics in the West Country, examines the major influences that shaped Jeremy Thorpe's life and surveys a career that came to a conclusion in a way that could hardly have been envisaged amid the successes of his earlier life.

Despite the fact that his father and maternal grandfather served as Conservative MPs, Jeremy grew up in a household where open minds were valued, and where family friends included the former Liberal Prime Minister and World War One leader, David Lloyd George and his children, Megan and Gwilym, who were later to become leading politicians in their own right and exerted a considerable influence on the young Jeremy.

The young boy's latent liberalism was further developed during the time he spent in the United States during World War Two, when he witnessed the campaign which led to the re-election of the Democrat Franklin Delano Roosevelt and imbibed the progressive atmosphere of Democratic New England. When Jeremy Thorpe went up to Oxford after the end of the war he became influential in the University Liberal Club and honed his debating skills in the Oxford Union, becoming Union President.

Whilst at Oxford Jeremy Thorpe led teams of Liberal students into action in various by-elections including, not surprisingly given the region's political history, contests in Devon and Cornwall. Here he came into contact with another hugely influential political family, the Foots of Plymouth. When Thorpe sought a constituency, the Foots guided his steps to North Devon.

The subsequent history of Jeremy Thorpe as MP and leader of the Liberal Party is an enduring part of the folklore of the West Country. His achievement and his legend, for his many admirers, are not tarnished by subsequent events.

1. Radical Politics and the West Country

Victory parades illuminated by the glare of flaming torches, snaking through the narrow streets of West Country market towns and fishing villages, boisterous eve-of-poll rallies where the fervent oratory matched that of Primitive Methodist camp meetings, and emotional slogans, inviting electors to vote for candidates who stood uncompromisingly for 'free trade, cheap bread and no protection'.

Radical politics in the South West peninsula traditionally threw up colourful candidates, like the pre-World War One member for Barnstaple, son of a wealthy Liverpool merchant with roots in the Portuguese colony of Goa in Western India, whose poll card read 'Vote for Ernest Soares and the Big Loaf'; Isaac Foot, Liberal Member of Parliament, staunch nonconformist in religion, and father of a famous brood of radical politicians and diplomats, and Richard Acland, who moved from a traditional Liberal stance to found a new far left party, and subsequently gave away his family's ancestral land holdings to the nation.

It all seems a long way from the political salons of Kensington and Knightsbridge, the playing fields of Eton College and the cloistered halls of Oxford academia, the milieu which nurtured the political ambitions of Jeremy Thorpe. Yet Thorpe, whose only previous connection with the West Country appeared to be a family seaside holiday in the North Devon resort of Woolacombe, fitted as naturally into the world of West Country liberalism as if he had been born and bred in the tradition.

The General Election of 1906 proved to be the high water mark of the twentieth century for the Liberals nationally and an equally memorable event for the party in the West Country. But in an era when the pace of life was considerably slower, communications were problematical in remote rural areas, and the boundaries of the United Kingdom's constituencies stretched to the west coast of Ireland as well as from Lands End to John O'Groats and beyond to Orkney and Shetland, voters had to be patient before learning the eventual result of the poll.

The election took place over a period of almost a month, from 12 January to 8 February. This is hard to believe for a twenty-first century electorate accustomed to exit polls producing fairly accurate forecasts of the result almost immediately the polling stations have closed their doors. The whole electoral process was much more random in the first decade of the twentieth century; the outgoing government set outside dates and left it to returning officers to organise the event.

When the 1906 overall results eventually did become known, there was jubilation in Liberal circles. On the electoral map both Scotland and Wales were largely solid for the party and a great deal of England was in the same condition. Only the counties which now form the Republic of Ireland represented a major contrast, being dominated by an Irish Parliamentary party dedicated to achieving home rule (the exceptions were mostly in the mainly Protestant north-east of the country).

No-one would have suspected as much at the time, but this was to be the last occasion on which the Liberals, led into the election by Sir Henry Campbell-Bannerman, won an absolute majority in the House of Commons; it was the last General Election too in which they won the popular vote. The Liberals elected 397 MPs to the 156 returned for the Tories, who were led by Arthur Balfour, with the Irish Parliamentary Party, under John Redmond, winning 82 seats.

An early warning to the Liberal party, although one unlikely to have resonated at a time of such great electoral triumph, was the fact that the Labour Representation Committee, the forerunner of the Labour party, led by James Keir Hardie, won 29 seats as opposed to just two in 1900. At an earlier stage in the history of the Labour Movement, Liberals and Labour had collaborated electorally, with those candidates who were essentially socialists being labelled 'Lib-Labs'. But once Labour realised they could win votes without Liberal support, they vowed to replace the Liberal party as the Parliamentary representative of the British working classes.

The 1906 election brought great joy to the West Country too. In later years the electoral map of the region was often to be coloured mainly Conservative blue, but in 1906 the South West peninsula's reputation as a Liberal stronghold was fully justified. Dorset, Somerset, Devon and Cornwall together returned 28 Members of Parliament; 23 of these were Liberals, including representatives of two double member constituencies in Devonport and Plymouth. There were just four Conservatives, in Dorset West, Taunton, Honiton, and Tiverton, and one Liberal Unionist, allied with the Conservatives, elected for Totnes.

In Barnstaple Ernest Soares, the sitting Liberal MP, saw his 1900 majority of 347, gained in a straight contest with a Liberal Unionist, rise to 2,045 over a Conservative opponent. Soares, who held the seat for eleven years from 1900, is believed to have been the originator of the spectacular torchlight processions which wound through Barnstaple following Liberal successes – a custom revived for Jeremy Thorpe's victories many years later.

Soares' flamboyance gave Barnstaple a foretaste of what was to come with Jeremy Thorpe. He was the son of José Luís Xavier Soares and the family were originally Brahmins, but converted to Christianity. Ernest Soares read law at St John's College, Cambridge and pursued a career as a solicitor. Whilst MP for Barnstaple he rented Upcott House, a large white stucco mansion just outside the town, from Sir William Williams of Heanton Court. Soares was a Junior Lord of the Treasury in the Liberal government of H. H. Asquith from 1910 to 1911 but in the latter year failing health forced his resignation from this post and from his Commons seat. He was knighted in the same year.

Another local Liberal victor in the 1906 election was George Lambert, MP for the South Molton division for 33 years from 1891 to 1924 and, after losing his seat to a Conservative in 1924, returned again at the 1929 General Election. Elected in '29 as a Liberal, he switched to the National Liberals in 1931 and continued to represent South Molton in that interest until 1945. Lambert sat in the House of Commons for forty-eight years, 348 days, ranking as the fifth longest-serving MP of the twentieth century.

When Lambert senior stepped down in 1945 and was created the 1st Viscount Lambert, his eldest son, also George Lambert, followed him as MP for South Molton and, when the seat was abolished in 1950, for Torrington. Initially, like his father in his later years, Lambert Junior stood as a Liberal National, although in his subsequent contests at Torrington he added the words 'and Conservative' to the description on the ballot paper. He succeeded his father as the 2nd Viscount Lambert in 1958.

If the scale of the Liberal triumph of 1906 has not, and seems unlikely ever to be repeated, there have been subsequent occasions when the counties of Devon and Cornwall have fully justified a reputation for radicalism, combined with nonconformism. There were times indeed when regional success allowed the party to forget that its overall national performance was less than spectacular.

Britain in the aftermath of World War One was politically far from stable, with four General Elections in the six years between December 1918, the so-called Coupon Election, held little more than a month after the Armistice, and the autumn of 1924. The country went to the polls in 1922, 1923 and again in '24.

The Liberal victor in 1906, Campbell-Bannerman, was succeeded as Prime Minister in 1908 by his Chancellor of the Exchequer, Herbert Asquith. It was Asquith who took a united country into World War One in 1914, but setbacks in the conduct of the war forced him into coalition with the Conservatives and Labour early in 1915. He was unable to weld the coalition into a really effective team, and he was overthrown by his fellow Liberal David Lloyd George, who replaced him as Prime Minister in December 1916.

For the 1918 General Election, Lloyd George's wartime coalition, riding on the euphoria of victory, agreed that certain candidates would be offered the support at the polls of the Prime Minister and of the Conservatives, led by Andrew Bonar Law. This support took the form of a letter, known as the Coalition Coupon, indicating the government's support of their candidacy. In the event, 159 Liberal candidates, 364 Conservatives, 20 candidates standing under the banner of National Democratic and Labour and two Coalition Labour candidates received a coupon.

A number of Conservative supporters, including Irish Unionists (this was the last election before Southern Ireland gained independence from Britain), and the Labour Party led by William Adamson fought the election independently, together with Liberals who did not receive a coupon. Lloyd George and the coalition won the election with ease, with the Conservatives the main victors as the largest party in the governing majority.

Most of the Liberals supporting the Lloyd George coalition government were elected. When Herbert Asquith had been deposed by Lloyd George in

1916 he had remained leader of the Liberal party. The faction supporting Asquith as opposed to Lloyd George was reduced at the election to just 36 seats and Asquith lost his own seat, at Paisley.

The coalition government re-elected in 1918 lasted until October 1922, when the Conservative MPs voted in favour of fighting the next election as an independent party, with its own leader and its own programme. Lloyd George was ousted as Prime Minister during the course of October in favour of the Conservative Andrew Bonar Law and the General Election followed on 15 November. Bonar Law carried the day, winning 344 seats. The Liberals were again divided, with the 'official' Liberal Party under Asquith winning 63 seats, an increase of 26 over the number won in 1918, while those who supported Lloyd George lost 74 seats compared to the Coupon Election, emerging from the contest with just 53 seats. The Labour Party, led by J. R. Clynes had 57 seats, the same number as in 1918.

Bonar Law did not live long to enjoy his triumph, resigning due to ill-health on 22 May 1923, after just 209 days in office. He was suffering from terminal cancer and died on 23 October that year, being succeeded by Stanley Baldwin, the Chancellor of the Exchequer. The Conservative Party, having won an election just a year before, could have waited for four years before calling another General Election, but Baldwin felt the need to be endorsed by the electorate.

His decision to call an election for 6 December 1923 backfired and he lost many seats to Labour and the Liberals. The ensuing Parliament was hung. The Tories had 258 seats, down 86 compared to the year before, whilst Labour, now led by Ramsay MacDonald had 191, a gain of 49. Before the election the Liberals had agreed to reunite and under the leadership of Asquith, with the blessing of Lloyd George, gained 43 seats to emerge with a total of 158. With no party having an overall majority, Labour formed a minority government.

Reunited and with a more than respectable total of seats in Parliament, although with the threat of being overtaken by Labour as the second political force in the country now a real possibility, the Liberals could allow themselves a modest amount of self-congratulation. In the West Country this took the form of a grand seven course banquet in the Assembly Rooms of the Royal Hotel in Plymouth on 23 February 1924, to celebrate the party's capture of the majority of seats in Devon and Cornwall at the previous December's election. The guest of honour was Herbert Asquith and the Liberal MPs from the two counties, including Tudor Rees, successful in the Barnstaple constituency, shared the high table with the former Prime Minister. Whether or not the spirit would have been as convivial as the menu and the wine list suggests, if the Liberals gathered together had realised what was to come within less than twelve months, is open to some doubt.

Labour's first spell in office lasted for less than a year, the minority administration falling as a result of losing a vote of no confidence in the House of Commons. The weary country went to the polls again – for the third time in less than two years – on 29 October 1924. The Conservatives gained a large Parliamentary majority of 209, Labour lost 40 seats and the Liberals lost 118 of the 158 seats they had gained as a reunited party the previous year. The effect was to polarise politics in Britain into a two-horse race between Conservatives and Labour.

Despite splits, election defeats and the spectre of the emergent Labour party, the Liberal faithful refused to lose heart. Among the guests at the Royal Hotel in Plymouth in February had been a man whose name was to become a legend in his own lifetime in the West Country, a politician who certainly never lost the Liberal faith. Isaac Foot, 44-years-old at the time of the celebratory banquet, was already one of the great names of nonconformism and radicalism in the West Country. He was the father of seven children, including four sons who were to make a substantial impact on British politics and public service throughout most of the twentieth century.

Another service rendered to the Liberal cause, nearly thirty years later, was to be the significant role Isaac Foot played in guiding Jeremy Thorpe's footsteps to a West Country constituency, when he might otherwise have looked for a seat in that other stronghold of Liberalism, Wales.

Isaac Foot was the son of a carpenter and undertaker, born in Plymouth in 1880 and educated at the Hoe Grammar School. He left school at fourteen and for a time worked at the Admiralty in London, before returning to Plymouth to train as a solicitor. He qualified in 1902 and, a year later, with his friend Edgar Bowden, founded the law firm Foot and Bowden, which as Foot-Anstey, still exists today. Foot joined the Liberal Party and in 1907 was elected to Plymouth City Council, remaining a member for twenty years. In 1920, as deputy mayor, he represented the city at the Mayflower tercentenary celebrations in the United States.

Like so many Liberal candidates in the twentieth century, Isaac Foot enjoyed both triumph and disaster in his quest for parliamentary status. He first stood for election at Totnes in 1910, losing to the sitting Liberal Unionist. He then fought Bodmin without success on two occasions, before transferring his candidacy to Plymouth Sutton in a by-election in November 1919. His successful Tory opponent in his own city was Nancy Astor, whose victory won her a place in history as the first woman to take her seat in Parliament.

After a dozen years of striving to gain a place at Westminster, Isaac Foot finally won Bodmin at a by-election in February 1922. He retained his seat in 1922 and 1923, only to be defeated in October 1924 – with the electors of Bodmin having endured four Parliamentary contests in the space of just over thirty months. At the 1929 General Election, which resulted in another minority Labour government under MacDonald, the Liberals won all five Cornish seats. Foot was back in Parliament for Bodmin, and this time he was to remain an MP for six years.

Ramsay MacDonald, faced with severe economic conditions, was forced to turn to budget cuts in areas unacceptable to the bulk of Labour MPs. He resigned in 1931 but was asked by King George V to form a National Government which comprised a rump of Labour members, including several ministers from the 1929 administration, the Conservatives and Liberals.

Isaac Foot was given ministerial office in the new government, as Secretary of State for Mines, succeeding the Labour politician Emmanuel 'Manny'

Shinwell. He served on the Round Table Conference on India in 1930-31 and Burma (1931), earning a reputation for his championship of the poor in the Indian sub-continent. His ministerial spell was short-lived however. As a convinced free trader, he resigned in 1932 over the protectionist Ottawa Agreements. Following his defeat at Bodmin in 1935 he was to fight two more Parliamentary elections, at St Ives in 1937 and at Tavistock in 1945, losing on both occasions.

Further distinctions were to come from other directions. Isaac Foot's Liberal principles stemmed in great part from his nonconformist background and he was Vice-President of the Methodist Conference in 1937-38. He was appointed Privy Counsellor in 1937, served on the Liberal party's National Council and was President of the party in 1947. One honour which brought him considerable satisfaction came in 1945, when he was chosen unanimously as Lord Mayor of Plymouth, despite not being a member of the council at the time.

Isaac and his first wife, Eva Mackintosh, had seven children, four of whom became distinguished public figures. The eldest, Dingle Foot, born in Plymouth, was educated at Bembridge School on the Isle of Wight and at Balliol College, Oxford, where he was President of the Oxford Union in 1928. Called to the bar in 1930 he practised not only in Britain but extensively in countries of the British Commonwealth. He was elected as the Liberal MP for Dundee in 1931 and during World War Two served Winston Churchill's wartime coalition government as Parliamentary Secretary to the Ministry of Economic Warfare.

At the first post-war general election in 1945 Dingle Foot lost his seat to the Labour candidate. He was adopted for the formerly Liberal seat of North Cornwall for the 1950 General Election, after the sitting member, Tom Horabin, had quit the Liberal Party to join Labour. Foot was defeated at the poll by a Conservative. In 1956 Dingle Foot himself left the Liberals to join Labour and won the Ipswich seat for his new party at a by-election the following year.

When Harold Wilson formed his first administration in 1964 Foot was made Solicitor-General, knighted and appointed to the Privy Council. He lost the Solicitor-General role in 1967 at a major government re-shuffle and then, at the 1970 General Election, was defeated at Ipswich by his Conservative opponent. Dingle Foot died in June 1978 in a hotel in Hong Kong, after choking on a bone in a chicken sandwich. He was 82.

The second of Isaac Foot's sons to gain prominence was Hugh, born in 1907 and educated at St John's College, Cambridge. He was President of the Cambridge Union and of the Cambridge University Liberal Club and his success at the Union mirrored the achievement of his three politically-active brothers in winning the comparative honour at Oxford – the other place'.

Hugh Foot's prominence came not so much in politics but in diplomacy, specialising in guiding former colonies to independence. However, after Labour's victory in the General Election of 1964, as Baron Caradon of St Cleer in the County of Cornwall, he became Minister of State for Foreign Affairs and British Ambassador to the United Nations. He died in Plymouth in 1990, at the age of 82.

The third of Isaac's sons was to achieve the most success in the political world, although falling at the final hurdle in a bid to become Prime Minister of the United Kingdom. Michael Foot was a Labour politician, journalist and writer, who was a Member of Parliament for a total of nearly four decades. He was a true West Country radical, who for much of his parliamentary career was at odds with his own party, at one stage losing the Labour whip. He nevertheless became Labour leader and leader of the Opposition when the party swung to the left after the 1979 defeat at the hands of Margaret Thatcher's Conservatives.

Michael Foot entered the House of Commons in his native city of Plymouth at the 1950 General Election, fighting and winning Plymouth Devonport. He held on to the seat in 1951 but lost in 1955 to a Conservative. Although he was never again to represent a West Country seat, he kept a lifelong attachment to Devon and was as passionate a supporter (and sometime director) of Plymouth Argyle Football Club as he was a socialist orator.

During his long political career he edited the left-wing newspaper *Tribune* and was one of the main disciples of the paper's founder, Aneurin Bevan. Foot was a leading 'Bevanite' until disagreeing with the Welsh politician over the issue of unilateral nuclear disarmament. Bevan refused to support this policy, famously arguing that he would not send a British Foreign Secretary 'naked into the conference chamber'.

Foot eventually wrote a two-volume biography of Bevan, the former miner renowned as the father of the National Health Service. And after Bevan's death in 1960 Foot succeeded to his Welsh valleys constituency of Ebbw Vale, remaining as MP for the division until the 1992 General Election.

Never caring to toe the party line regardless, Michael Foot lost the Labour whip in 1961 through a dispute over defence spending, not regaining it until 1963 when the left-leaning Harold Wilson became leader of the party following the death of the right-wing Hugh Gaitskell. Wilson offered Foot a place in his 1964 government, but this was turned down, Foot preferring to lead the left from the back benches. He was a difficult man for a Prime Minister to deal with in his own party, following his principles, opposing attempts to limit immigration and being one of the leaders of Labour opposition to membership of the Common Market.

When Labour returned to power in 1974 after the defeat of the Edward Heath government and the failure of an attempt to gain Liberal support to keep Heath in power, Foot accepted a Cabinet role as Secretary of State for Employment, an appointment designed to keep the trades unions onside. Unlike some politicians whose more extreme views mellow as the years pass, Michael Foot continued to be firmly on the left of the Labour party. After the party's 1979 General Election defeat and the subsequent resignation as party leader of deposed Prime Minister James Callaghan, Foot became Labour leader in November 1980, a compromise candidate giving the party a choice in addition to the more mainstream contenders, Denis Healey, Peter Shore and John Silkin.

Foot was already 67 on his election to the party leadership. Britain was in recession and the Thatcher government had inherited the problems caused by trades union militancy which had contributed to the downfall of Callaghan. With unemployment mounting, Labour moved ahead of the Conservatives in the opinion polls and the election of a Devonian radical as Prime Minister looked increasingly possible.

Foot, who the author met when the politician was given an honorary degree by The University of Nottingham (for his literary merit, rather than his political achievements) came across very often as a shambolic character, untidy in appearance and despite his intellectual standing, also gave the impression of being badly organised. When the author asked Foot for a copy of the notes of his address to the degree ceremony, the Labour leader complied, but the notes were so rambling (and virtually illegible) as to be unusable.

The Conservative politician Kenneth Baker commented that 'Labour was led by Dixon of Dock Green under Jim Callaghan. Now it is led by Worzel Gummidge.' The nickname was gleefully adopted by the right-of-centre press and there was also the incident of the Remembrance Day ceremony at The Cenotaph in Whitehall, when Foot was accused by newspapers of insulting the war dead by turning up wearing what was described as 'a donkey jacket.' The garment was actually a rather expensive form of duffle coat. It was not only the Conservatives who joined in the criticism; one Labour MP likened Foot's appearance to that of 'an out of work navvy'.

The formation of the Social Democratic party – which formed an alliance with the Liberals in 1981 and was later to merge into the Liberal Democratic party – whittled away Labour support and the popularity among the public of Margaret Thatcher's decision to send a Task Force to re-capture the Falkland Islands after their seizure by Argentina in 1982 (Foot supported the military action) made a Conservative General Election success in 1983 more or less a foregone conclusion.

The Labour party manifesto for the 1983 election, dubbed as 'the longest suicide note in history', embracing unilateral nuclear disarmament and other far-left policies, did not help matters and Foot was soundly defeated at the polls. Michael Foot resigned four days after the defeat, being succeeded as leader by Neil Kinnock, who began the march back to the centre for the party which was completed by Tony Blair. For the remainder of his time in the House of Commons, Michael Foot took a back seat. From 1987 to his retirement in 1992, he was the oldest sitting British MP.

In many ways Michael Foot was a complete contrast to his father Isaac – Labour rather than Liberal, an atheist as opposed to a staunch Methodist and a committed republican, but one cannot help thinking that Isaac would have been proud of his son's enduring radicalism and his unwavering adherence to the principles he had established for himself at the start of his career. Michael Foot died in March 2010, aged 96.

The fourth politically active son of Isaac Foot was John Mackintosh Foot, born across the Tamar from Plymouth at Pencrebar, Callington. After Oxford and the Foot tradition of achieving the Presidency of the Union, he joined the family law firm and eventually became senior partner. John Foot was considered by his brother Michael to be the best orator and ablest member of the family. However, his own political career was unsuccessful. Loyal to his father's Liberal views, he stood for Parliament on four occasions, including twice in Isaac's old stamping ground of Bodmin, but was never elected.

He remained true to the Liberal party during its long twentieth century decline and was made a Life Peer in 1967 as Baron Foot of Buckland Monachorum in the County of Devon. He chaired the UK Immigrants Advisory Service from 1970 to 1978 and criticised the Wilson government for what he believed was its inadequate fulfilment of pledges to the persecuted Kenyan and Ugandan Asians. He also fought for the preservation of Dartmoor against what he regarded as the expansionist ambitions of Plymouth City Council, ironically the authority which had been his father's launch pad into a political career. John Foot died in 1999, aged 90.

Another famous West Country radical who, like Dingle Foot and others began life as a Liberal, was Richard (later Sir Richard) Acland, the scion of a wealthy landowning family, whose Parliamentary career began when he fought and won Barnstaple in 1935, defeating the Conservative candidate Benjamin Lampard-Vachell, who had been adopted for the seat after the sitting Tory member, Basil Peto, retired from Parliament. Acland became one of 33 Liberal MPs elected at the 1935 contest, two fewer than the number of Liberal Nationals.

In 1935 the Liberals, despite their modest return of seats, could still be reckoned as a truly national political party. The 33 seats were widely distributed across Britain, from Caithness and Sutherland in the far north to North Cornwall (held by Richard Acland's father, Sir Francis Acland) and North Devon in the south west, and from the Isle of Ely in the east to Merioneth in the mountains of North Wales.

In the larger industrial towns and cities the Liberals won seats in London, at Bethnal Green, in Bristol, Birmingham, Birkenhead, Dundee, Middlesbrough, Paisley and Wolverhampton., whilst in the West Country Barnstaple and North Cornwall were in the hands of the Acland father and son combination.

Richard Acland, a Devonian, born at Broadclyst in 1906, was the son of Francis Dyke Acland, the 14th holder of the Baronetcy of Columbjohn and the sitting Liberal MP for North Cornwall. Richard was educated at Rugby School and Balliol College, Oxford, was admitted as a barrister at the Middle Temple in 1930 and served as a lieutenant in the Royal Devon Yeomanry. The younger Acland's first and unsuccessful attempt at being elected to the House of Commons came at Torquay in 1929. He switched to Barnstaple for the 1931 General Election, but was defeated by the sitting Conservative Basil Peto. When four years later Acland again fought Barnstaple and won the seat, he became the constituency's first Liberal MP for 12 years.

Although strong-minded and farther to the left of the political spectrum than many, perhaps most, of his Liberal Parliamentary colleagues, there were initially no indications that Acland would be anything more than a dutiful member of the party at Westminster and his abilities were noticed by the party leaders, who appointed him a junior whip. An early indication of his future career path was when he began to advocate closer ties with the Labour party and electoral co-operation with them at constituency level.

Acland's political stance began to take a steady turn towards the left. He was heavily influenced by the rise of Fascism in Italy and Germany, and the 1936 coup in Spain, where the initially faltering attempt by military leaders to overthrow the democratically-elected government in Madrid quickly developed into a full scale civil war, in which the rebels, eventually led by General Francisco Franco won military support from Hitler and Mussolini. The main support for the Madrid government came from the Soviet Union, whilst other powers, led by France and Britain, endorsed a non-intervention pact, blocking arms to the Spanish Republic.

The Soviet Union encouraged co-operation across the European mainland between socialist, social democratic and communist parties, under the banner of the Popular Front, with the aim of opposing the dictators and furthering the USSR's own long-term aims. In the late 1930s Acland helped to launch the UK's version of the Front, urging an alliance between political parties and individuals of the left and centre-left, in a bid to challenge the policy of appeasement of the Fascist powers adopted by the Prime Minister of the era, Neville Chamberlain (but opposed by many, including the future wartime leader Winston Churchill).

In the perennially moderate United Kingdom, the Popular Front (PF) was met with suspicion in many quarters on the political left. It failed to gain the formal endorsement of either the Labour party or the Liberal party. There was no General Election during this period to test the potential overall support of the PF and its likely ability to become a political power in the land. The founders of the Popular Front in the UK were Acland, John Strachey, a Communist and former MP, the Labour intellectual and economist G. D. H. Cole and the progressive Conservative MP Robert 'Bob' Boothby.

The Labour party opposed the Popular Front from 1938, although it was initially supported by the Labour-affiliated Co-operative party. Co-operative party chairman Alfred Barnes, also a post-war minister in the Attlee government, personally endorsed the Popular Front and the party conference at first voted in favour of the movement, although it later changed its stance.

The first time the Liberal party formally considered the Popular Front was at a meeting of their executive committee on 20 October 1936, when members received but rejected a proposal to support the movement submitted by the writer and philosopher Aldous Huxley. The executive did not think that an electoral pact with Labour was possible or even desirable. At a subsequent meeting of the ruling party this position became official Liberal policy. In April 1937 the issue was debated at the Union of University Liberal Societies Conference and once again the Popular Front was rejected.

There is little hard evidence to suggest what the officials of the Barnstaple Constituency Liberal party thought of the pro-Popular Front activities of their young MP.

In the late 1930s the English, Scottish and Welsh universities still had parliamentary representation. At the Combined English Universities by-election in 1937 the former Liberal MP Thomas Edmund Harvey gained the seat from the Conservatives standing as an Independent Progressive, seeking to rally antigovernment supporters on the left. The success of this campaign caused many left leaning academics to consider if candidates standing under a similar platform could be as successful in non-University seats.

The Popular Front issue came closer to North Devon via the Bridgwater by-election in November 1938. The impetus for action came from Barnstaple MP Richard Acland, who approached Vernon Bartlett, a journalist and broadcaster with extensive experience of foreign affairs to stand as an anti-appeasement candidate. Bartlett agreed to do so providing he had the support of the Liberal and Labour parties. Taking a similar line to Acland, the Bridgwater Liberal party unanimously backed Bartlett's candidature.

Securing Labour's co-operation proved more difficult. Before the by-election vacancy was known, the local Labour party had already re-adopted Arthur Loveys, their previous candidate, to contest a General Election expected to occur in 1939. Loveys withdrew and Labour generally supported Bartlett, although some Labour voters were reluctant to support him, believing that in reality he was a Liberal candidate. However, he did receive a letter of support from 39 Labour MPs just before polling day and duly won the seat with a majority of 2,332.

Richard Acland's championship of the Popular Front came even closer to home in 1939, when he turned his attentions to the Tiverton constituency, which had been a solid Conservative seat since the Tories took it from the Liberals in 1924. No Liberal or Labour candidate had stood in the seat since 1929. The Liberals had however selected a candidate in 1939 to fight the next General Election.

At this point Richard Acland's father, Sir Francis, the Liberal member for North Cornwall, took a hand in the proceedings. Sir Francis Acland had represented Tiverton in parliament in 1923, winning the seat at a by-election and retaining it at the General Election that year. As a result he had a strong influence with the Tiverton Liberal Association, which was open to the idea of supporting an Independent Progressive candidate, if such a candidate were supported by the local Labour party.

The Tiverton Liberals believed a member of the party, Michael Pinney, would appeal to Labour locally. By March 1939 Pinney had agreed to stand as a Popular Front candidate and the previously adopted candidate had agreed to withdraw in his favour. In April 1939 the local Liberals and the local Labour Party both formally endorsed Pinney, but in May 1939 the national Labour authorities put an end to the Popular Front activity in the Mid-Devon town by overriding the local party.

Calls for a Popular Front ceased when Britain declared war on Nazi Germany. However, it was increasingly recognised that during wartime, it was better to have a broad- based government that could command all-party support. By May 1940 Winston Churchill had become Prime Minister and included in his new government other Conservative anti-appeasers and the leaders of the Labour and Liberal parties. The Communist party's support for co-operation fluctuated depending on the foreign policy of the Soviet Union. In 1940 one of the main Popular Front protagonists, Stafford Cripps, was appointed by Churchill as Ambassador to the Soviet Union.

In 1942 Acland finally severed his connection with the Liberal party and his Barnstaple Constituency Association, and spent the rest of the war years sitting in Parliament as a member of his new party, Common Wealth. One of his main associates was the novelist and playwright J. B. Priestley, well known during World War Two for his radio talks, designed to boost morale among the British public. Another of Acland's lieutenants was the Communist Tom Wintringham, who had honed his fighting skills on the Republican side in the Spanish Civil War and was appointed by Churchill's government to teach guerrilla tactics to the Home Guard.

Common Wealth opposed the wartime truce between the major parties, which took the form of not contesting by-elections which occurred when sitting Members of Parliament died or retired. The new party did contest by-elections and won three. When normal politics resumed in 1945 Acland, having burnt his bridges in North Devon, stood for Common Wealth in Putney. The momentum had gone from the new party however. Just one MP was elected and Acland himself could only manage third place in Putney.

Acland then joined the Labour party and was selected to fight Gravesend . He won a by-election in the Kentish seat in November 1947 but became disillusioned with Labour in 1955, resigning from the party in protest against the party's support for the Conservative government's nuclear defence policy – Acland was one of the founders of the Campaign for Nuclear Disarmament (CND). He lost the Gravesend seat when he stood as an Independent, allowing the Conservatives to win the constituency at the expense of the new Labour candidate.

In 1944 Acland, an advocate of public land ownership, gave his West Country estates at Killerton in Devon and Holnicote in Somerset to the National Trust. He became a teacher, lectured in education at St Luke's College, Exeter, retired in 1974 and died at 83 in 1990.

The first General Election since 1935 – one was scheduled for 1940 but not held, because of World War Two – was called for 5 July 1945, two months after VE Day but before VJ Day, which followed in August. Polls in some northern constituencies were delayed until 19 July, because of local wakes (holiday) weeks. The results were counted and declared on 26 July, to allow time to transport the votes of those serving overseas.

With Acland now standing (unsuccessfully) for Common Wealth in Putney, the Barnstaple Liberals selected a member of a prominent political family to try and hold the seat they had gained in 1935 and which remained Liberal up to Acland's defection to Common Wealth in 1942. Mark Bonham Carter, aged 23 in 1945, was the son of the Liberal activists Sir Maurice Bonham Carter and his wife, the former Lady Violet Asquith, daughter of the Liberal Prime Minister H. H. Asquith. Educated at Winchester College and Balliol College, Oxford, his studies were interrupted by the Second World War, and he was commissioned into the Grenadier Guards in November 1941. Captured in Tunisia in 1943 and imprisoned in Italy, he escaped and walked 400 miles to return to British lines, being mentioned in dispatches.

The Conservatives fielded a candidate with an equally distinguished war record in the form of Christopher Henry Maxwell Peto, a younger son of Sir Basil, MP for Barnstaple from 1922 to 1923 and again from 1924 until he retired from politics at the 1935 General Election. Christopher Peto served in both of the twentieth century's World Wars and reached the rank of Brigadier during World War II, when he was awarded the DSO.

Despite the tide swinging against the Conservatives, Peto had a majority of just over 4,000 over Bonham Carter. The result nationally was an unexpected landslide victory for Clement Attlee's Labour party, over Winston Churchill's Conservatives. It was the first time the Conservatives had lost the popular vote since the 1906 election; they would not win it again until 1955. Labour won its first majority government, and a mandate to implement its post-war reforms. The 12.0% national swing from the Conservative party to the Labour party remains the largest ever achieved in a British general election.

The Labour candidate in the three-horse race for the Barnstaple seat, Ivor Williams, reflected the swing to Labour by gaining more than 10,000 votes and recording nearly 25 per cent of the total vote. Christopher Peto was to hold the North Devon seat in 1950 and 1951, before retiring from politics. But politics in the northern part of the county of Devon was yet to hear more of the names Bonham Carter and Peto.

The 1945 General Election had seen the Liberals, led by Sir Archibald Sinclair, minister for air in Churchill's wartime coalition government, elect 12 MPs. The party lost nine seats, including Sinclair's constituency of Caithness and Sutherland, and Barnstaple. In the West Country as a whole the Liberals retained North Cornwall and Frank Byers, later a life peer and Liberal leader in the House of Lords, gained the formerly Conservative seat of North Dorset.

Between 1945 and 1950 Labour, for the first time governing with an overall majority, achieved many of the objectives it had set out in its manifesto, notably the establishment of the National Health Service, the granting of independence for India and Pakistan, and nationalisation of the railways, the steel industry and other concerns.

But it had fallen to the lot of the Attlee government to be in power during the difficult immediate post-war years for a Britain impoverished by the costs of waging war for six years. The austerity imposed by Labour proved unpopular and at the 1950 General Election Attlee just squeezed back into power with the narrow majority of five seats, despite polling over 700,000 votes more than the Conservatives and receiving more votes than they had in the landslide 1945 victory.

The 1950 contest, held on 23 February, produced a new low for the Liberals, both nationally and in the party's traditional stronghold of the West Country. Led for the first time by Clement Davies, the MP for Montgomeryshire in Mid-Wales, the party lost three seats, reducing its total in the House of Commons to nine. Not a single seat was won in Devon, Cornwall, Somerset or Dorset. The only representatives of radical politics in the region were Labour, successful in Falmouth and Camborne and in the Plymouth constituencies of Devonport and Sutton.

The Liberal party had fielded 475 candidates in 1950, more than at any general election since 1929. Clement Davies felt that the party had been at a disadvantage in the public's perception at the 1945 general election when they ran fewer candidates than needed to form a government. Davies arranged for the cost of running extra candidates to be offset by the party taking out insurance with Lloyd's of London against more than fifty candidates losing their deposits. In the event, a total of 319 Liberal candidates lost their deposits, a record number until 2015, when candidates for the Liberal Democrats lost 335 deposits at the general election held in that year. The rump of surviving Liberal MPs illustrated the fact that the party was no longer a national force. Five of the nine members were from Wales and three from Scotland. The sole English MP was Donald Wade from Huddersfield.

Worse was to follow for the Liberals. The 1951 general election was held twenty months after the 1950 contest. Attlee's Labour government could struggle on no longer with its tiny majority. Once again Labour won the popular vote but the Conservatives had the most seats and gained an overall majority of 17. Under the constituency boundaries as defined at the time, Labour piled up huge majorities in safe seats but were unable to hold on to marginals. This election marked the beginning of the Labour Party's thirteen-year spell in opposition, and the return of Winston Churchill as Prime Minister.

This time the Liberals, again led by Clement Davies, won just six seats and in all but one case, these victories were due to electoral pacts with the Conservatives. Donald Wade was joined by another successful candidate from the north of England, Arthur Holt from Bolton. Both Huddersfield and Bolton were double member constituencies and in the seats held by Wade and taken by Holt, the Conservatives gave them a free run against Labour. Of the remaining four Liberals, the three from Wales, Roderic Bowen from Cardigan, Rhys Hopkins Morris from Carmarthenshire and Clement Davies from Montgomeryshire, also benefitted from electoral pacts. Only Jo Grimond from Orkney and Shetland could be said to have won his seat without assistance.

In North Devon the party suffered the humiliation, never experienced before or since, of coming third behind the Tories and Labour. After the smoke of the election had cleared there were again no Liberal seats in the South West. The region represented a sea of Tory blue with the sole exceptions of the Labour wins in Falmouth and Camborne and in Michael Foot's Plymouth Devonport. Plymouth Sutton, won by Labour in 1950, on this occasion fell to the Conservatives. In North Devon Christopher Peto increased his majority from 6,084 in 1950 to 9,148 and his share of the vote rose from 46 to 52 per cent. The Liberal candidate, Alexander Halse, polled 7,326 votes compared to the 11,640 his predecessor Guy Naylor had obtained in 1950, with the Liberal vote share declining from more than 30 per cent to less than 20 per cent.

Labour had a particularly strong candidate in William 'Bill' Wilkey. He was an Alderman of Barnstaple Borough Council, an authority he had first joined in 1932, serving until 1938 and then standing for election again and becoming a fixture on the council in the 1950s and 1960s, helping to push through the authority's slum clearance programme. Wilkey's 10,632 votes gave him a 28 per cent share of the total votes cast. The result he achieved, which cast local Liberals into gloom, remains Labour's best-ever performance in North Devon, notwithstanding the period from 1974 to 1983 when the seat included Bideford and rural areas around that town and the total electorate was much higher than in 1951.

As 1951 faded into 1952, the outlook for the North Devon Liberal Association looked bleak indeed. But help was close at hand. A clever, stylish and charismatic young man, with the polish of an Eton and Oxford education but with an absolute commitment to Liberal principles, had decided to apply to become North Devon's prospective Liberal Parliamentary Candidate.

Jeremy Thorpe was on his way and nothing would ever be the same again in North Devon.

Postscript:

It is interesting to note that the three most notable radical politicians produced by the West Country in the twentieth century had one thing in common; they rose to positions of eminence but failed to achieve the glittering prize of the post of Prime Minister of the United Kingdom, a role they undoubtedly all coveted.

The career of Michael Foot, leader of the Labour party and Leader of Her Majesty's Opposition, reached the final hurdle, with the Plymouth man leading his party (albeit disastrously) into a General Election in 1983.

David Owen, born in Plympton was a Plymouth MP from 1966 to 1992. His first unsuccessful attempt to win a seat in the House of Commons was at Torrington in 1964. At the 1966 General Election he won the Plymouth Sutton constituency from the Conservatives and in February 1974 became MP for the adjacent Plymouth Devonport seat, defeating the sitting Conservative, Dame Joan Vickers by fewer than 500 votes. He retained the seat in October 1974 and in 1979. From 1981 his involvement with the Social Democratic party – he was one of the 'Gang of Four' who broke with Labour – meant that he had developed a large personal following and he was re-elected with safe margins until receiving a peerage in 1992. Owen, a medical doctor, was the youngest man to hold the rank of Foreign Secretary and was widely tipped as a future Labour leader and possible Prime Minister.

Jeremy Thorpe, the only one of the three not to have been born in Devon, dreamt from childhood of restoring the fortunes of the Liberal party and achieving the personal status and power once held by his political hero, David Lloyd George. He is acknowledged to have laid the foundations for the Liberal revival which reached a peak in 2015 when the party, with more than 50 MPs, held the balance of power (another of Thorpe's dreams) and entered into coalition with David Cameron's Conservatives. But for the long-festering scandal which overtook him in 1979, would Jeremy Thorpe have gone on to lead a Liberal revival in his own right and be esteemed as an elder statesman?

2. Thorpe's Road to Devon

The atmosphere at the first meeting of the North Devon Liberal Association following the 1951 General Election was grim. In the smoky committee room at the Liberal offices in Cross Street, Barnstaple, above the bar of the Liberal Club where sorrows had been drowned in the days following the contest, the executive of the Association were still struggling to come to terms with the fact that their candidate had slipped to third place in the poll behind the victorious Conservative and the Labour runner-up..

The fortunes of the Liberals nationally had been in decline ever since the party had last won an absolute majority in the House of Commons in 1906. At the first General Election following World War Two, held in July 1945, the party elected just 12 MPs. In 1950 that figure fell to 9 and when Britain went to the polls again in 1951 Liberal representation in the House slumped to just six members.

The old Barnstaple Parliamentary constituency (replaced by North Devon for the 1950 General Election) had alternated over the years between the Liberals and the Conservatives. Since the date generally accepted as seeing the birth of the modern era in politics, 1885, up to the division's abolition in 1950 and replacement by the new North Devon seat, the Liberals had held the seat for a total of 34 out of 65 years, compared to the 16 years when it had been in the hands of a Conservative member.

The Liberal Unionists, who had split from the main party over the issue of Home Rule for Ireland (and generally supported the Conservatives) had held Barnstaple for a total of 11 years and Richard (later Sir Richard) Acland, elected as a Liberal in 1935, broke with the party in 1942 and spent the last three years of World War Two sitting as a member of the new left-wing party he created, Common Wealth.

At the first election after the creation of the new North Devon constituency, in 1950, the seat went to the Conservative, with the Liberals in second place. Then came the poll in 1951 and humiliation, when a strong local Labour candidate, Alderman Bill Wilkey, forced the Liberal contender into an unprecedented third place.

With the party's fortunes at such a low ebb both nationally and locally, the small band of Liberal loyalists at the party meeting were in despair. But Jack Prowse, a party activist who had helped to carry Richard Acland shoulder high down Barnstaple High Street on the last occasion a Liberal won the seat, was made of sterner stuff. As his youngest son and political activist Malcolm recalls today: "My father told me that there was talk of simply winding up the Liberal organisation in North Devon and giving in – it seemed that bad to many people. But dad agreed to take on more of the work and said his wife, my mother Lilian, would be willing to do a few jobs, typing letters and that sort of thing!

No one could have realised it at the time, but the decision to keep going taken that evening in 1951 would form the foundation for the construction of a constituency organisation unrivalled anywhere within the party. Lilian Prowse herself would become one of the finest full-time constituency agents in twentieth century British politics. Giving it another go would also bring to North Devon a man who would put the constituency firmly on the British political map.

It could be argued that Jeremy Thorpe was born with a House of Commons pass almost within his grasp. The political life was certainly deeply embedded in the family psyche. His father, John Henry Thorpe, had spent some years in the House of Commons, albeit before Jeremy was born. His mother, Ursula, the daughter of another Conservative Parliamentarian, Sir John Norton-Griffiths, was herself politically active in the Tory cause.

If the family exerted a strong and traditional Conservative influence – Thorpe's maternal grandfather was nicknamed 'Empire Jack' because of his passionate imperialism – then other influences were present during the years when Jeremy was growing up. Although John Henry Thorpe's time as an MP had been brief – he sat for the Rusholme division of Manchester from 1919 to 1924 – he maintained many contacts in the political world, both within and outside the party he had represented in the House of Commons.

Although no Thorpe was sitting in Parliament during Jeremy's most formative years, the household was deeply political. Jeremy's own political dreams and ambitions were nurtured in very different locations, far removed from the sunken lanes, turbulent sea coasts and barren moorland heights of the West Country constituency that was to be his political power base and, later, his retreat from the cares of political scandal and illness, for more than six decades, from his first introduction to the constituency in 1952 to his death in 2014.

His first exposure to politics came within the household. Jeremy's first home, following his birth in 1929, was deep in the heart of professional upper middle class London, in a spacious and fashionable terraced house in Onslow Gardens, South Kensington. His parents moved house when he was just four years old, to the even more fashionable address of Egerton Gardens, Knightsbridge. Despite the economic recession of the 1930s and the poverty and despair it created through large swathes of industrial Britain, the child's world, growing up with parents and two older sisters, was one of comfort and security, with a large staff of servants, including nannies for the children, on attendance upon the family.

In keeping with his adult life, when those who knew him well recall that, despite his apparently opulent lifestyle, he was always short of money, the circumstances of his parents' life also represented something of an illusion . John Henry, known within the family as Jack or 'Thorpy', and Ursula Thorpe had little capital and lived to the fullest extent of their income.

The child of a political family, living close to the 'Westminster bubble', Jeremy was exposed to politics and politicians from a very early age. 'Thorpy' had friends at a high level within the Conservative party, which as a result of the steady post-World War One decline of the Liberals and the failure of the Labour Party to maintain stable administrations in the 1920s and the early '30s, dominated the child's early years, governing as firstly the dominant element in Ramsay MacDonald's National Government post 1931 and then, from 1935 to the outbreak of war in 1939, as the overwhelming party.

Friends of Jack Thorpe held high office in both the National Government, and ministers and their wives were frequently entertained at the family home. Despite this strong Conservative background, by far the greatest political influence on the young Jeremy was to stem from the Thorpes' close friendship with the Lloyd George family. At first sight, this appeared to be a strange relationship, given that Jeremy's maternal grandfather, John Norton-Griffiths, 'Empire Jack' was, as the nickname suggests, an aggressive colonialist and no friend of David Lloyd George. In his turn, Jeremy's father, as a Conservative MP, had helped to vote the legendary war leader out of office in 1922.

The inter-family relationship was built on the close friendship between Ursula Thorpe and Lloyd George's daughter, Megan, and to a lesser degree on the fact that during the Parliamentary sessions of 1922, Jack Thorpe had formed an inter-party friendship, common at Westminster, with Megan's brother, Gwilym Lloyd George, then a Liberal MP. On the birth of a son for Jack and Ursula, Megan Lloyd George became Jeremy's Godmother.

As a result of the friendship between the families, the backcloth to Jeremy's political education changed from time to time from the stylish London setting to the rugged landscape of North Wales where, from the mid-1920s onwards, the Thorpes spent holidays with Megan and Gwilym at Brynawelon, the Lloyd-George's family home near Criccieth, in the historic county of Merioneth (now Gwynedd). The presiding force at Brynawelon was David Lloyd George's wife, Dame Margaret, who had been largely superseded in the former Prime Minister's life and affections by his secretary and mistress, Frances Stevenson (whom he was later to marry).

Despite the rupture within the Lloyd George family, Jeremy Thorpe came into contact with the politician and statesman, both at his London home and at Bron-y-de, his country house in Churt, Surrey. Jeremy's first encounter with David Lloyd George came in 1935 when, having recovered from tuberculosis, the child was allowed to accompany his parents on their annual excursion to North Wales. It has been estimated that Jeremy and the former Prime Minister met on up to a dozen occasions, and despite Thorpe's youth, he was captivated by the personality of the one-time Liberal leader. Slight as they may have been, Jeremy's contacts with David Lloyd George ensured that the Welsh politician was to prove a life-long role model and political hero.

If the aura that surrounded David Lloyd George made a deep impression on the youthful susceptibilities of Jeremy Thorpe, a much more substantial contribution to his political outlook was undoubtedly made by Megan Lloyd George, who by the time Thorpe came into close contact with her family was already an active Liberal politician.

Born in 1902, Megan became the first female member of Parliament for a Welsh constituency when she won the Anglesey seat in 1929. Throughout her political career she was heavily influenced by her father and like him she refused to support MacDonald's National Government in 1931, standing at the

General Election that year as one of a small group of Liberals who stood alongside her father in opposition to the official party line. She re-joined the Liberal fold in 1935 and represented Anglesey for the party until 1951. Her views moved steadily to the left and during World War Two she was a member of a group called Radical Action, which, like Richard Acland's Common Wealth party, campaigned for a more radical stance on the part of the wartime coalition government and for the Liberal party to withdraw from the electoral truce of the period, under which the main political parties agreed not to contest the by-elections that occurred from time to time.

As a Welsh patriot Megan Lloyd George also campaigned for a Welsh Parliament and for the appointment of a Secretary of State for Wales, moves which years later Jeremy Thorpe was to support as an MP and leader of the Liberal party. She grew to consider that the Liberal party was moving away from the radical politics which had been her father's hallmark and cultivated a friendship with Labour Prime Minister Clement Attlee.

She was elected as Deputy Leader of the Liberal party in 1949, in a move designed to strengthen party loyalty, but after losing the Anglesey seat stood down from the post. In 1955 she joined the Labour party and stood against the Liberals in Carmarthen, where she was successful in winning the seat, which she held until her death in 1966 at the age of 64. Her defection to Labour was a blow to Jeremy Thorpe, by now himself a Liberal candidate in North Devon. He later told his biographer Michael Bloch that he felt 'shattered and bitter' at Megan's defection; nevertheless, he did not allow it to destroy his friendship with his Godmother.

As the prospect of a second world war grew closer, the Thorpe family moved out of stylish metropolitan London to an equally fashionable rural location, the village of Limpsfield on the Surrey-Kent border, quintessential southern England, the spot where the North Downs meet The Weald. Once hostilities were actually declared in September 1939, the Thorpe parents settled into war work, Jack Thorpe becoming personal assistant to a Member of Parliament serving at the Admiralty whilst Ursula became billeting officer for the Limpsfield District, finding accommodation for those people whose living arrangements had been dislocated by the conflict.

Jeremy, now 10 years old, was sent to a local school as a weekly boarder and, unlike his previous experience at a preparatory school he disliked intensely, soon settled down. The circumstances of war were soon to cause the greatest upheaval he had experienced so far in his short and generally secure life. His father's name appeared on the notorious Nazi blacklist of those people involved in British public life who would be eliminated as a matter of urgency should the Germans succeed in invading and subjugating the British Isles.

Jack Thorpe, and members of his family, were considered to be vulnerable to Nazi threats because of Jack's work on alien tribunals, which had undertaken the task of deciding who were genuine asylum seekers (including many over the years fleeing from Nazi persecution) and those who were actually under-cover spies.

The decision was taken to send Jeremy and his sister Camilla to live in the

United States, with their American aunt, Kay Norton-Griffiths. Evacuation of children from families with contacts across the Atlantic was commonplace; former Labour minister Shirley Williams, later to be one of the founders of the Social Democratic Party (SDP) and later leader of the Liberal Democrats in the House of Lords, was evacuated to Minnesota for three years. Jeremy was sent to the Rectory School in Pomfret, Connecticut. Like his early political contacts with the Lloyd George family, this was to prove a seminal point in the development of his character and views.

Rectory was a (relatively) progressive and liberally-minded educational establishment in New England, the most progressive and liberally-minded region of the USA. Those who came to know him well in later years believe his years at the school and his exposure to Democratic Party politics, and in particular the beliefs and policies of President Franklin D. Roosevelt (whose election for a third term occurred during Jeremy's American schooldays), cannot be overestimated. One theory is that this influence was not so much a result of the ethos of the school but because of Jeremy's reaction to the views of his classmates, who mostly came from conservative, Republican backgrounds,

In 1943, with the threat of a German invasion of the British Isles now long past, it was felt that it was safe for children to return home, although they still had to negotiate the German U-boat threat during the Atlantic crossing. Jack Thorpe used his political connections to secure for Jeremy a passage in the Royal Navy cruiser HMS *Phoebe*.

On his return to Britain Jeremy was sent to Eton College, where most sources agree that his career was less than distinguished, apart from his developing skills with his violin. Traditionalists disliked, among other things, his decision to avoid service in the College Cadet Force. The subject of Jeremy and military service was to re-emerge not long after his farewell to Eton. Happily for him, the final crucial location for his political inspiration, Oxford University, was to prove much more congenial and rewarding.

Thorpe left Eton in March 1947 with a place to read law at Trinity College, Oxford, secured for a future date. First of all he had to undertake 18 months National Service, an obligation which led to a curious incident. His career in the armed forces actually only lasted for a few weeks before he was discharged on medical grounds. Thorpe had apparently collapsed whilst attempting an assault course. Some commentators believe the collapse was staged, with Thorpe unwilling to put his political ambitions on hold.

With his university place not available until the following year, Jeremy filled in the gap by working as a temporary teacher at a preparatory school before going up to Trinity in October 1948. The college was founded in the sixteenth century as a training house for Roman Catholic priests but became a pillar of the Anglican establishment in the seventeenth and eighteenth centuries and a centre of educational reform in the nineteenth.

Its list of distinguished alumni includes figures as diverse as the playwright Terence Rattigan, the actor Nigel Davenport and the McWhirter brothers, Ross and Norris, who founded the *Guinness Book of Records* and edited the publication until Ross was murdered by the Provisional IRA. Famous statesmen and politicians from Trinity include Muhammad Ali Jinnah, the founder of Pakistan, Lord North, British Prime Minister during the American War of Independence, who served in both Whig and Tory administrations, the Whig politician and Prime Minister Pitt the Elder and, in more recent times, Labour's Anthony Crosland, perhaps best known for his implacable opposition to grammar schools when Secretary of State for Education and Science in the 1960s. Somerset MP Jacob Rees-Mogg is one Trinity graduate currently active as a (Conservative) politician and the College also contributed to the education of King Philippe of Belgium.

On arrival at Trinity, Jeremy Thorpe made a conscious decision to forego the glittering prizes offered by pure academic success and instead build the power base he believed would propel him into the political career that had been his overriding ambition from an early age.

The dandyism and flamboyant behaviour that was already such an important part of Thorpe's persona had not been greatly appreciated at Eton; at Oxford it was to prove an essential part of his campaign to be noticed. Michael Bloch, whose autobiography of Thorpe is essential reading for anyone interested in the man and not just in the later troubles that led to the Old Bailey dock, writes that Thorpe's 'pallid appearance, dark hair and eyes and angular features, gave him a *'diabolonian air'.

Jeremy's desire for a political career, and more specifically his decision to pursue that career path in the Liberal party, led to his joining at the earliest opportunity the Oxford University Liberal Club (OULC). Although the Liberal party nationally was at its lowest ebb in the immediate post-World War Two years, the OULC was surprisingly strong, with more than 800 members in 1948.

The club was founded in 1913, formed from two older Liberal societies at Oxford, the Russell Club and the Palmerston Club, both dating back into the 1870s. The new OULC had the declared aim of 'rallying progressive members of the University to the support of Liberal principles.' Like the party itself, the club experienced ups and downs and, reflecting the situation in the political world, lost much ground to the newly-established Oxford University Labour Club in the 1920s. Splits in the Liberal ranks were mirrored at the University, with the establishment of the New Reform Group, a pro-Lloyd George organisation.

Ironically, the best period for the OULC prior to the immediate post-World War Two period had been in the mid-1930s, when the driving force was the club's treasurer, the future Labour Prime Minister Harold Wilson. Wilson was aided by the club President Frank Byers, who was to win the North Dorset constituency for the Liberals in the 1945 General Election. Byers was appointed Liberal chief whip but lost the seat at the 1950 General Election and never re-entered the House of Commons. When Wilson became Prime Minister for the first time in 1964 Byers was made a life peer and in 1967 became leader of the Liberals in the House of Lords.

Jeremy Thorpe wasted little time in making an impact on the OULC. By the

*A disciple or worshipper of the Devil, in the works of John Bunyan

end of his first term at the University he had become a member of the club committee and in November 1949 became President. Under his enthusiastic leadership membership increased to an unprecedented 1,000 members. Jeremy was active in Liberal affairs not just at Oxford, and helped to increase his reputation as a coming man by working in the party's election campaigns across the country, organising groups of student Liberals, known as 'University Commandos' to stiffen the ranks of local activists wherever there was thought to be a good chance of a victory for the party.

On reaching his 21st birthday (the age at which young people received the vote at that time) Thorpe became eligible to place his name on the Liberal Party's list of potential Parliamentary candidates, and duly applied.

The fact that the OULC had become increasingly noted for its social activities did not reduce its importance in Thorpe's eyes. An important part of his career strategy was the making of contacts, for which a wider and often diverse membership served him very well.

These contacts and the establishment of a reputation word of which was spread through the relatively small world of British politics and public life also flourished through the medium of the Oxford University Law Society and, more crucially, through the Oxford Union, a renowned debating society recognised as a stepping stone to prominence in both politics and other fields.

Jeremy Thorpe enjoyed swifter success in his quest for office in the Union than most other aspirants. It was generally the custom that those aiming for the Presidency should serve first in the organisation's other principal offices – of secretary, treasurer or librarian. Thorpe, a forceful debater, full of self-confidence, stood directly for the top job in 1950 but was defeated by the future television journalist (and Liberal party member) Robin Day. The setback was short-lived.

Although Day beat Thorpe to the post of Union President, Jeremy was to come out top in terms of politics. Robin Day stood unsuccessfully as a Liberal at Hereford in 1959, the year that Thorpe won North Devon. Day was on record in his later years as regretting that he had never entered Parliament, although for many years his abrasive interviews with politicians, especially during General Election campaigns, meant that his contributions to political life were more significant that those of many who did achieve election.

Thorpe had approached his first Union presidential campaign in his usual no-holds barred manner. Although this approach was not to everyone's taste, it brought him notice and this paid off later in 1950 when he achieved his goal, beating the future Labour MP Dick Taverne and the Conservative William Rees-Mogg, subsequently editor of *The Times* newspaper and the father of the aforementioned Tory MP for North Somerset, Jacob Rees-Mogg.

Dick Taverne, now Lord Taverne, a Liberal Democrat peer, was to play a leading role in what is seen as a major realignment in British politics. In the 1970s, as the sitting MP for Lincoln and in dispute with his local party over his support for what was to become the European Union, he quit Labour and resigned his seat, winning the subsequent by-election in the cathedral city as the Independent Democratic Labour candidate. He held his seat in February

1974 but lost it in October of that year. He became a member of the Social Democratic Party (SDP) and after the merger of the SDP and the Liberals joined the Liberal Democrats.

Jeremy Thorpe's term as President of the Oxford Union has gone down on record as one of the liveliest in the history of the distinguished body. Among the speakers he attracted to Union debates was the Conservative cabinet minister and Lord Chancellor Quintin Hogg, later Lord Hailsham. Hogg was also noted for his flamboyance, a fact which was probably not lost upon Thorpe when compiling the list of speakers.

There was inevitably a price to pay for Jeremy as a result of his time-consuming range of extra-curricular activities at Oxford. He needed an additional fourth year to complete his Law studies and when he graduated in the summer of 1952 it was with a third-class honours degree.

Having already secured a place on the Liberal party's list of potential candidates, Thorpe was interviewed by the party's candidates committee in April 1950, whilst still an undergraduate in just his second year at Oxford. It has been suggested that his precocious talents led the committee to consider him as a future successor to the Welsh barrister and politician Clement Davies, who led the Liberal party from 1945 to 1956. Davies held what was considered to be the party's safest Parliamentary constituency, Montgomeryshire, but was just 66 and unlikely to give up his political career in the near or medium term. Thorpe was not inclined to be patient in his search for a seat.

Montgomeryshire in 1952 was certainly a plum for any aspiring Liberal politician. Clement Davies, first elected in 1929, left the party temporarily to join the ranks of the Liberal Nationals, supporting the 1931 National Government of Ramsay MacDonald and later supporting the Conservative administration which came to power at the 1935 General Election. On both the latter occasions Davies was unopposed and when he returned to the ranks of the Liberals in 1945, he was returned in a straight fight with the Tories. In 1951 and 1955 he was not opposed by Conservative candidates and easily disposed of the Labour opposition. By 1959 he had been replaced as Liberal leader by Jo Grimond and, this time facing a Tory candidate, saw his majority considerably reduced. Davies died in 1962.

Jeremy Thorpe did take some lessons in the Welsh language from Megan Lloyd George, but his Parliamentary ambitions were to focus on the other side of the Bristol Channel. One of the seats where the Oxford University Liberal Club concentrated its firepower at the 1950 General Election was North Cornwall, where the sitting member Tom Horabin had outraged the party by defecting to Labour three years earlier. Jeremy's leading role in the fight for North Cornwall, at the head of the Oxford 'University Commandos, brought him into close contact with the Foot family, the political clan already encountered in Chapter 1, *Radical Politics in the West Country*. A developing friendship was to have far-reaching consequences for Thorpe's career.

Tom Horabin was selected for North Cornwall in 1939, following the death of sitting Liberal Sir Francis Acland. Along with the then party leader, Sir Archibald Sinclair, he was a vocal opponent of Prime Minister Neville

Chamberlain's Nazi appeasement policy. Horabin won the 1939 by-election against the Conservatives and after he had been re-elected in 1945 was appointed chief whip by Clement Davies, then the new party leader.

Horabin nevertheless soon became concerned about what he saw as the pro-Conservative sympathies of some Liberal MPs. In 1946 he gave up the Liberal whip to sit as an independent, going one step further and accepting the Labour whip in the following year. He was urged by North Cornwall Liberals to resign and fight a by-election but refused, saying that he still stood for the principles outlined in his election address in 1945.

For the 1950 contest Labour invited Horabin to contest North Cornwall on their behalf. Again his maverick nature became apparent and he refused to stand on the grounds that he would be campaigning against people who had previously worked for him. Horabin had been seriously injured in an aeroplane crash in 1947 and he also argued that contesting the scattered North Cornwall seat would put too much of a strain on his health.

The Liberals fielded Dingle Foot, eldest son of the Foot family patriarch Isaac, himself a former MP and President of the Liberal party. When the country went to the polls it was the Conservative candidate who emerged as the victor, with a five and a half thousand majority over Dingle Foot. Labour finished a poor third. Dingle Foot was to fight the seat again at the 1951 General Election, again coming in second place.

Ironically, given the local party's experiences with Horabin, Dingle Foot was also to defect to Labour, in 1956. He returned to the House of Commons in 1957 for his new party and held office in Harold Wilson's 1964 administration.

The Foot connection, cemented during the North Cornwall contest, served to persuade Jeremy Thorpe that his future lay in the West Country rather than in Wales or any of the other rather limited areas of the country where the party still had a chance of winning seats. The West Country certainly wanted the services of Jeremy Thorpe, with interest in a possible candidacy being shown by Torrington and North Cornwall. But Dingle Foot's agent had strongly recommended Thorpe to the Liberals in North Devon, and the local association, recovering its confidence under the leadership of Jack Prowse, was impressed by Jeremy's track record at Oxford and his activities as an enthusiastic worker in the field.

Thorpe's political stance at the time of his adoption matched that of other young Liberal activists, who believed that the party should offer a radical non-socialist alternative to the Conservative government. He and others founded the Radical Reform Group, to drive the party in that direction.

Jack Prowse and his fellow Liberal officials in North Devon saw Thorpe as a natural successor to their former MP Ernest Soares, who had shown similar elements of charisma, exhibitionism and flamboyance. Thorpe quickly exhibited his showmanship, imitating the North Devon dialect (exactly) and showing an interest in the constituency's concerns.

The Liberal position at the time was actually worse that the 1951 General Election total of just six elected Members of Parliament suggested. This lowly figure soon declined to five MPs, as the death of one of the six resulted in a loss at the subsequent by-election.

Such was the state of affairs when Jeremy Thorpe was adopted as Liberal Prospective Parliamentary Candidate for North Devon. Thorpe, then and throughout his active political career, dreamt of leading the great Liberal revival, in which he had a passionate belief. He did not lead it, did not benefit from it, but undoubtedly made it possible. When he first visited North Devon in 1952 many of the party's slim band of activists were living on the memories of past glories,

The question being asked in party circles was whether the new candidate could not only reclaim the second place at the polls forfeited in 1951 but go further and actually win the seat? Malcolm Prowse takes pride in recalling not only the glory days to come but also the foundation on which they were based.

"You could say that the Liberal revival that Jeremy Thorpe was dreaming about at Oxford started the day Dad refused to give in, and volunteered Mum's services too!"

3. At Home in the House of Commons

Some men and women, despite a burning ambition to succeed in national politics, nevertheless suffer a negative reaction when they actually find themselves *in* the House of Commons.

They find it a strange and often baffling place, with its arcane rituals, the contrast between the combative and occasionally abusive atmosphere within the debating chamber and the many strong cross-party friendships between individual MPs and, not least, the cramped surroundings and the strange fact that the Mother of All Parliaments, unlike most legislative assemblies across the globe, is unable to seat all of its members on full-dress occasions.

Jeremy Thorpe, when he finally made it to Westminster, immediately felt at home. It was not just the fact that he was continuing the family tradition which had seen his father and maternal grandfather occupy the green benches of the Commons chamber, or the presence of close friends from the Lloyd George and Foot families. Most of all it was for Thorpe simply a logical step towards realising the ambition, nurtured from an early age, of leading his party and restoring it to its old glory and pre-eminence.

Adoption as the Prospective Liberal Parliamentary Candidate for North Devon was just the first step on a road that Thorpe was absolutely confident would lead him to great things. His confidence and self-belief never faltered, despite the fact that a long seven years were to elapse between his introduction to the North Devon constituency and his first election to Parliament.

Gaining a seat at Westminster, by no means a simple matter for a Liberal in the 1950s, was for Thorpe one step on the ladder to a political career. At all times he was looking ahead, way beyond simple constituency success. From the moment his political dreams began to take solid shape, Jeremy had no intention of becoming a simple foot soldier in the severely denuded ranks of the post-war Liberal party. The party as a whole, across the United Kingdom and in North Devon, might be in a state of near despair, with a concentration on mere survival, but Thorpe was never likely to accept such a defeatist attitude.

His attachment to the Liberal party was much more than a childish romantic dream nurtured by the Lloyd George connection, nor was it an undergraduate fad, but a real commitment, stemming from a true belief in the tenets of Liberalism. Long before his adoption as candidate for North Devon he had begun to assiduously woo any politician or official within the Liberal party who could assist what he undoubtedly saw his as his future rise to party leadership, an essential step if he was to fulfil his role at the head of a major revival in the party's fortunes.

At the time Jeremy formed his connection with North Devon, there were many within the Liberal ranks whose commitment wavered from time to time.

When Winston Churchill, a former Liberal himself, returned to 10 Downing Street in 1951 he set out to entice leading Liberals into the Conservative fold, via a series of moves which, had they been successful, would have effectively meant a merger of the two parties.

When Churchill was forming his government in the immediate aftermath of the 1951 contest, there was an offer of a cabinet post for Liberal leader, Clement Davies, and the post of Lord Chancellor was suggested for former Prime Minister Herbert Asquith's son Cyril. Both offers were rejected, with Davies afterwards hinting that a telegram from the Oxford University Liberal Association had been a major factor in his rejection of the honour. The Lloyd George family had suffered in the '51 contest, with Jeremy's Godmother and close friend Megan Lloyd George losing her Anglesey seat. Although Megan was to regain the seat and remain a Liberal until 1957, this was one stage in the ongoing flirtation with socialism that was eventually to lead her into the Labour party.

Megan's brother Gwilym sat as Liberal MP for Pembrokeshire from 1922 to 1924 and again from 1929 to 1950, although by the late 1940s he was effectively an Independent Liberal in alliance with the Conservatives. At the 1950 General Election he was defeated by the Labour candidate but returned to the House of Commons a year later as Liberal and Conservative MP for Newcastle-on-Tyne North. He had held ministerial posts during Churchill's wartime coalition but now, having moved solidly to the right politically, he became Minister of Food (1951-54) and Home Secretary and Minister for Welsh Affairs (1954-57). As Home Secretary he refused to commute the death sentence passed on Ruth Ellis, the last woman to be executed (for murder) in the United Kingdom.

In the 1950s Jeremy Thorpe saw his earliest political friends and allies either depart the scene or gradually move away from the Liberal party. His hero, David Lloyd-George, died in 1945, Gwilym was now a minister in Conservative governments and Megan was toying with defection to Labour. In the Foot family, Isaac, although still a loyal Liberal, was no longer politically active and Dingle, largely responsible for guiding Jeremy towards North Devon, was to join Labour in 1956.

But whilst others wavered, Thorpe concentrated his boundless energy and the political skills he had honed at Oxford on re-building Liberal strength in North Devon. After Thorpe's death, paying tribute at his funeral in 2014, Nick Harvey, then Liberal Democrat MP for North Devon, described Jeremy as "the personification of hope (for the Liberal Party) when it was needed most. Nobody should overlook his fierce and unwavering commitment to Liberal principles."

A similar line was taken by *The Times* journalist Julian Glover. Writing on the *Liberal History Website*, Glover said: "Thorpe's persistence with the party, when he could have succeeded as a left-leaning Conservative or as a Labour candidate, points to a commitment to Liberalism greater than critics have claimed."

Even before his adoption for the North Devon seat, Thorpe had been marked down by many within the Liberal party hierarchy as a (perhaps as *the*) coming man. His work for the Oxford University Liberal Club and his enthusiasm for and skill in campaigning was clearly going to be noticed in a political organisation largely moribund and hardly overwhelmed with applications for membership or candidatures by young men and women of Thorpe's exceptional potential.

After his adoption as candidate for North Devon, Thorpe was elected as a member of the National Liberal Club on the proposal of Dingle Foot, still at that point within the Liberal fold. The club, like its Tory equivalents, performed the dual role of a gentleman's club and a venue for meetings and other gatherings, where those in control of Liberal fortunes in a time of decline could debate how to save the party, watched over by the portraits of predecessors who had known real political power.

He spent a great deal of time in North Devon, cultivating the personal approach to the voters that was to become his trademark. He skilfully mixed attention to purely local concerns with his conspicuously liberal views on larger international issues.

Winston Churchill's post-war spell as Prime Minister lasted from the end of October 1951 to 7 April 1955. On the latter date, aged 80 and aware that he was slowing down both physically and mentally, Churchill resigned and was succeeded by Anthony Eden, who had been Foreign Secretary in the wartime coalition and had held the post again since the Tories returned to power in 1951.

A General Election followed quickly, on 26 May 1955. Political historians have described it as one of the 'dullest' electoral contests of the post World War Two era. The Conservatives won a substantially increased majority of 60 seats, against a Labour Party perhaps too preoccupied with infighting between its left and right wings to offer a coherent and vote-winning alternative message to the Conservative claims that their re-election was essential to the continuance of the gradual economic recovery from the war years.

Despite the presence on the list of candidates of Jeremy Thorpe, the 1955 contest in North Devon apparently matched the national campaign in its dullness. The campaign in the constituency was charitably described in one newspaper as being 'the most tranquil in local history, with little happening to disturb the quiet organisation of all parties.'

Journalists had to wait until a few days before the eve of poll for an incident to enliven the proceedings. The Conservative candidate, James Lindsay, rushed out a nationally-produced flyer featuring an image of Labour leader Clement Attlee with Aneurin Bevan, the former Minister of Health, who was the right-wing media's bogey man of the time – the predecessor of Tony Benn, Ken Livingstone and others; the Tory flyer insisted 'You cannot have a united Britain led by a divided party'. On the reverse side of the sheet was what was coyly described by the press as 'a reference to the Liberals' inability to form a government.'

Tame as it might seem today, the flyer brought complaints from both Jeremy Thorpe and the Labour candidate, Harold Heslop, who described it as 'bad form and bad taste'. Lindsay countered by quoting a strip cartoon issued by the

Liberal party nationally, depicting a donkey with the caption , 'Don't be a silly ass and vote Labour'; a mule, captioned 'Don't be a stubborn mule and vote Tory' and, finally, a horse, with the legend, 'Use horse sense and vote Liberal'. This pamphlet, said Mr Lindsay, accused the majority of North Devon electors of being 'either asses or mules.'

The North Devon Liberal Association denied any responsibility for the flyer, with Thorpe telling the press that it had been ordered without the authority of his election agent or himself. He added: "The moment we discovered that an independent person had been sent a stock of these, I ordered every one of them to be destroyed."

On polling day Lindsay held the seat for the Conservatives but Jeremy Thorpe succeeded in reducing the majority from 9,148 to 5,226 on a night when the swing to the Tories across the country was two percent. The North Devon Liberals were pleased with the result, declaring it to be 'a great moral victory' and Thorpe himself told the crowds who had gathered to hear the declaration: "We have given the Tories the biggest hiding of any constituency, bar none", adding: "We have started on the long road back."

The chairman of North Devon Liberals, Mr A. W. Hughes, described the result as 'very satisfactory' and added that the party had every intention of adopting Thorpe as candidate again.

The progress the North Devon Liberals had made on all fronts since the appointment of Thorpe as prospective candidate in 1952 was a vindication of the party's concentration on what the press had dubbed 'quiet organisation'. During the four years following the 1955 contest, the Liberals worked even harder to extend the party's network of branches, which also served as efficient fund-raising bodies.

When Britain went to the polls again for the 1959 General Election, the number of bodies on the ground wearing Liberal rosettes, many of the helpers being enthusiastic Young Liberals, should have acted as an early warning for James Lindsay and the local Conservatives. If the campaign had been far livelier than in 1955, the result of the poll and the fervour of the Liberal celebrations in Barnstaple following the count at the Queen's Hall, provided headlines in plenty.

Senior Liberal activists knew victory was theirs several minutes before the public declaration of the result. They were reported as having rushed to the glass doors separating them from the expectant crowds packing Boutport Street, with the majority waving mauve and yellow favours. Pandemonium broke out when the returning officer, F. J. Broad, walked out on to the balcony of the Queen's Hall. The noise abated just long enough for him to start detailing the candidates and the votes cast in their favour. He managed to speak the word 'Thorpe' but was instantly drowned out by 'a deafening roar'. The time of the balcony appearance was recorded as 11.40pm; it was almost midnight before North Devon's new MP could make himself heard above the cheering.

Some of the crowd then made their way home without knowing the margin of Thorpe's victory over Lindsay – just 369 votes. What mattered for most of the people in the street was the fact that a Liberal had won the division for the first time for 24 years. When the excitement had eased a little, Thorpe was allowed to make his victory speech, followed by comments from James Lindsay and Harold Heslop.

The majority of the crowd was in no mood to go home, determined to be part of local political history. When Jeremy Thorpe came down into the street he was quickly hoisted on to the shoulders of supporters and chaired from the Queen's Hall, down Butchers' Row and across to the Liberal Club. On arrival at his headquarters he appeared at a window and introduced some of his main helpers, and his mother, Ursula Thorpe, to the boisterous crowd who had followed him from the count.

"This is not my victory," he shouted. "It is your victory," before announcing that the Liberal Club had invested in 18 gallons of Devonshire cider – "just in case they might be needed." The press reported that it was 1am before the celebrations at the Liberal Club ended.

The newly elected MP observed the proprieties and paid due tribute to his two opponents. But he wasted little time in making it crystal clear that he was not going to Westminster to sit on his hands. He told the still cheering crowds: "I look upon this as a declaration of war on unemployment in this area and as a cry from the countryside to see that we bring services to those in our rural areas. I appreciate now that the hardest work lies ahead of me and I only hope that I can prove worthy of the trust you have out in me. The future of the people of this division means as much to me as anything in my life."

On the evening following the declaration of the result Liberal supporters gathered again in Barnstaple to celebrate the victory. They met in North Walk soon after tea, with a steady stream of cars and buses bringing in reinforcements from the surrounding areas of the constituency. Just before 7pm, the crowds marched to Sticklepath, on the far side of the River Taw, where Jeremy Thorpe was waiting to lead the throng in a victory parade across the Long Bridge and back into the centre of the town.

The marchers were headed by a yellow banner inscribed with the word Victory in black letters, which had been used in 1935 when the seat had last fallen to the Liberals. The press reported that those following the banner included many teenagers or men and women in their early twenties. About four hundred carried flaming torches. Crowds six or seven deep lined The Square and broke into loud cheers as the torches could be seen crossing the bridge.

The eventual destination of both Thorpe and the crowds was the Pannier Market, where the new MP kissed his mother, Ursula, and greeted the architect of his victory, agent Lilian Prowse. There were few dissidents on the night but one man, presumably a Labour supporter, was heard to make the bitter remark that the first three letters in the word VicTORY might just as well have been obliterated.

Not too far away from Barnstaple, there were similar scenes of jubilation in Torrington. This time however, the cheers were for the Conservative candidate, Percy Browne, who had beaten Mark Bonham Carter and regained the seat the Liberal had held for just 18 months since the 1958 by-election triumph. The media reported that jubilant Tories danced in the street at Torrington, whilst at

Bideford, supporters waited on the quay for the victor, against a background of exploding skyrockets.

Once all the cheering had died down the local press got down to some detailed analysis of what the two very different results meant for the area. The victors, Jeremy Thorpe and Percy Browne, now formed the youngest pair of MPs on record for the two constituencies in the geographical area of North Devon. Browne was 35 and Jeremy Thorpe just 30. The district found itself in the unusual situation of having changed both of its MPs without having altered its party representation in the House of Commons; the Conservatives made their only gain of the election at Torrington and the Liberals made their only gain from the Conservatives in North Devon. The election, said one commentator, should go down in local history as the 'all change – no change' contest. It is unlikely that Jeremy Thorpe would have endorsed the claim of 'no change'.

Thorpe's flamboyance, a reputation in the national Liberal Party far in excess of the standing accorded to a new MP – even to one who had achieved the Party's sole General Election victory of 1959 – his prominence as a regular face on television at a time when there were just two channels, claiming the allegiance of many millions of viewers, had ensured that it was not just the local and regional press watching the North Devon result.

In 1959 the Conservative-supporting *Daily Express* was one of the most influential voices in the country. Political commentator William Barclay, writing just days after the result was declared, said: "It will be a shocker to see a sign of life among the Liberals, but I am assured that the old eyes will see it in Jeremy Thorpe."

The heavyweight *Observe*r, on the Sunday after the election, linked Thorpe's name with those of two other faces familiar to TV viewers who had won Parliamentary seats for the Tories – the athlete Christopher Chataway and Geoffrey Johnson Smith. Thorpe, said the *Observer*, was 'the most striking of the television victors'.

When the 1959 General Election became yesterday's news, Lilian Prowse and her fellow Liberal officials hardly needed reminding that, triumph thought it undoubtedly had been, Thorpe's majority was very small. Much work would be needed if North Devon was to become anything more than an outright marginal.

If 1959 marked the beginning of the Parliamentary career of a future party leader, it also saw the zenith of the political life of the overall victor in the election, Harold Macmillan, the originator of the claim that 'our people have never had it so good' and dubbed by the Tory press as 'SuperMac'. Over the next four years Macmillan's reputation was to become tarnished by economic troubles and scandal.

Declining popularity led Macmillan to sack no fewer than seven of his cabinet colleagues in one fell swoop in July 1962, described by the press as 'The Night of the Long Knives'. Jeremy Thorpe, who was to become both admired and feared in the House for his wit, gained instant notice when he adapted a Biblical phrase and, summing up the mood in Westminster, declared: "Greater love hath no man than this – that he lay down his friends for his life."

By October 1963 Macmillan had come to believe that he was seriously, perhaps even terminally, ill. He resigned and was replaced by the 14th Earl of Home, who had been Leader of the House of Lords and Foreign Secretary in Macmillan's administration. By the mid-1960s it had become politically unacceptable for a Prime Minister to sit in the Lords. Home renounced his peerage and was introduced into the safe Unionist seat of Kinross and West Perthshire in Scotland. Parliament's new session was delayed until after the necessary by-election, which Home, who for 20 days had been Prime Minister while a member of neither House of Parliament, won comfortably, taking his seat and place at Number 10 Downing Street as Sir Alec Douglas-Home.

Home led the government for under a year and called a General Election for 15 October 1964. Labour's new leader, Harold Wilson, who succeeded to the post on the death of his predecessor, Hugh Gaitskell, won a narrow majority of just four seats. The Liberals, under Jo Grimond, increased their haul of seats from six to nine and in North Devon Thorpe increased his majority from a precarious 369 to the rather more comfortable figure of 5,136.

A remarkable record of electioneering in North Devon at the 1964 General Election exists and is available to view online (*see details at the foot of the page*). Westward Television, which held the West Country commercial TV franchise at the time, put together a 20 minute programme reviewing the events of the campaign and the eventual results in two constituencies, North Devon and Bodmin. Both recorded Liberal victories at the election, through Thorpe in North Devon and, ironically given later events, Peter Bessell in Bodmin.

The programme was introduced and linked by Westward TV reporter and later well-known West Country political figure, David Mudd, who was later to hold the traditionally Labour or Liberal seat of Falmouth and Camborne for the Conservatives, from 1970 until 1992. Mudd launched the documentary sitting on the riverside at Barnstaple, near The Athenaeum, with the Long Bridge in the background.

The scene shifted to South Molton, where in his voice-over Mudd showed pictures of semi-derelict properties, claiming that a major fall in population was one of the problems facing the North Devon constituency. A shot of elderly men in flat caps sitting on a bench outside what was then the Midland Bank in South Molton square emphasised the influx of retired people into North Devon.

Staying in South Molton, the scene moved to the old sheep pens, lying between East Street and the livestock market. The film featured the two contenders for Thorpe's seat, the Conservative Michael Peto and the Labour candidate Frank Paton, introduced to viewers as himself a farmer in Somerset. On this occasion Jeremy Thorpe was not to be seen in the market, instead being filmed in wellington boots and customary smart suit, talking to workmen carrying out flood prevention work on the River Yeo in Barnstaple.

The film can be viewed at: https://player.bfi.org.uk/free/film/watch-jeremy-thorpe-and-peter-bessell-1964-1967-1964-online

Jeremy Thorpe is seen later in the film meeting local people in the Barnstaple Pannier Market and in Butcher's Row. Several minutes of the film switch the action to Bodmin in the aftermath of Bessell's victory. The size of the crowds celebrating his win prove that Liberal fervour was by no means limited to North Devon during the era.

A 'tour de force' insertion into the film from later in the decade proved to be the well-known 'takeover' by Thorpe of Landkey Post Office, allowing the husband and wife team who ran it to go away for their first holiday in many years. The interviewer for this segment of the programme was Clive Gunnell, pictured talking across the counter to Jeremy, who was resplendent in a long brown shopkeeper's cotton coat, of the type later made famous by comedian Ronnie Barker in the TV series *Open all Hours.*

Gunnell suggested to Thorpe that many people were saying that his decision to take over the running of the post office was simply a rather obvious electioneering gimmick. Thorpe, always a match for a TV interviewer given his own experience in the field, replied that such was not his intention, adding: "I suppose anything a politician ever does can be claimed to be a publicity stunt."

The film offers a perfect opportunity to gain a snapshot of electioneering in the mid-1960s. Little of North Devon and Cornwall life as depicted in the programme gives much hint that the nation was on the cusp of the Swinging Sixties, Beatlemania and, more pertinently, of social reform including the legalisation of homosexual relations between consenting adults.

Harold Wilson's first government, with its unworkable majority, was in power for 17 months. Wilson then called a snap election for 31 March 1966 and easily defeated the Conservatives under their new leader Edward Heath, gaining a majority of 96 seats. Nationally the Liberals again increased their Parliamentary representation, with three gains taking them to a total of 12 MPs at Westminster. Jeremy Thorpe, facing a determined new Conservative opponent, Tim Keigwin, a local farmer and landowner, saw his majority slip from more than 5,000 to 1,166. Throughout his 20-year tenure as MP, Thorpe's majority fluctuated.

When Britain went to the polls again, in 1970, he would not only have to defend his unpredictable seat but also lead a national campaign, having in the interim having been elected leader of his party.

Above: Radical politics. Ernest Soares was the Liberal MP for Barnstaple from 1900 to 1911. He rivalled Jeremy Thorpe for charisma and flamboyance and introduced the torchlight victory processions later adopted by his successor. *(Prowse family)*

Devon and Cornwall Liberal Federation.

DINNER

In Celebration of the Liberal Victories in Devon & Cornwall,

ASSEMBLY ROOMS, ROYAL HOTEL, PLYMOUTH, on

SATURDAY, FEBRUARY 23rd, 1924,

At 6-45 p.m.

Principal Guest:—The Right Hon.

H. H. ASQUITH, K.C., M.P.

Supported by the Liberal Members of Parliament in the two counties.

SIR FRANCIS LAYLAND-BARRATT, BART., will preside.

Left: A banquet was held in Plymouth to celebrate the Liberal party's success in Devon and Cornwall at the 1923 General Election. Former Prime Minister Herbert Asquith was guest of honour and signed the programme. The Barnstaple MP Tudor Rees was also in attendance. *(Prowse Family)*

A very young Jeremy Thorpe in 1953, just months after his adoption for North Devon, meets party activists at a Liberal fête at Bestridge, Swimbridge. *(Mervyn Dalling)*

Above left: Wooing the farming vote in his early years in North Devon. Jeremy Thorpe meets, from left, farmers Reg Thorne, Kenneth Waldon and Jim Yeo. The occasion is probably the annual flower and garden show at Chittlehampton. *(Gerald Waldon)*

Above right: Jeremy Thorpe as he appeared to the electorate of North Devon when he first won the seat in 1959. *(North Devon Liberal Association Archive)*

The Kingmakers. Jack Prowse, who in 1951 persuaded the North Devon Liberals to carry on after the party's worst-ever defeat and his wife Lilian, who became full-time agent for the constituency in 1958 and masterminded seven election victories for Jeremy Thorpe. Lilian is wearing the pearls given to her by Jeremy to mark her contribution to his success at the polls. *(Prowse Family)*

Left: Liz Prowse and Jeremy Thorpe at a constituency dinner. *((North Devon Liberal Association Archive)*

The Young Liberals were a power in North Devon under the leadership of David Worden, pictured canvassing with a fellow member. *(David Worden)*

'I mean the LIBERAL PARTY can help YOU'

Says Mr. ALBERT SAMPSON, of Mariansleigh, South Molton.

"We farm workers have never gone on strike to improve our conditions; but there's a lot to be done if we're going to stop this endless drift to the towns. Liberals want farm workers to get wages as good as those in other industries; they also favour creating more opportunities for farm workers to become smallholders and eventually small farmers.

"All these things would be made possible by the Liberal plans for a prosperous agriculture. North Devon's agriculture needs a Liberal M.P. next time."

Make it a Liberal, North Devon!

Above right: Lilian Prowse used the views of authentic Liberal voters to put across the party's policies to the electorate, in an extensive advertising campaign. Farmer Albert Sampson spoke with the voice of the farming community. *(North Devon Liberal Association Archive)*

As party membership increased the North Devon Association flooded the streets of the constituency with activists. Liberals of all ages prepare to canvass in Northam. *(North Devon Liberal Association Archive)*

Support from the top. The then Liberal leader Jo Grimond came to North Devon to support the campaigning Jeremy Thorpe.
(North Devon Liberal Association Archive)

The North Devon Liberals staged a mass rally in Barnstaple's historic Pannier Market in October 1969 to celebrate the first ten years since Jeremy Thorpe's election as a Member of Parliament. *(North Devon Liberal Association Archive)*

Jeremy and Marion Thorpe head the victory parade in Barnstaple after Thorpe's record majority in the 1974 General Election. Lilian Prowse is prominent on the left of the picture, with Mrs Ursula Thorpe by his side. *(R. L. Knight)*

A family man. Jeremy and his first wife Caroline, with their son Rupert, at their cottage near Cobbaton, in the North Devon constituency. *(North Devon Liberal Association Archive)*

A political helper. Caroline Thorpe with Colne Valley MP Richard Wainwright at a constituency dinner in North Devon. *(North Devon Liberal Association Archive)*

Thorpe spent many hours meeting his loyal voters, like the members of a quiz team pictured here. At the MP's right shoulder, as always, is his agent Lilian Prowse. *(North Devon Liberal Association Archive)*

Jeremy and his second wife, Marion, pictured at the North Devon cottage.
(North Devon Liberal Association Archive)

4. Ambition Fulfilled: Thorpe as Liberal Leader

Jeremy Thorpe saw his election to the House of Commons in 1959 as but a preliminary step towards fulfilling his ambition to lead the Liberal party to new glory. Some aspiring politicians might well have decided that the immediate priority was to consolidate the position in their constituency; 369 votes was hardly a comfortable majority in a seat that had been comfortably held by the Conservatives since the end of World War Two in 1945. But caution was a word which hardly existed in Jeremy's vocabulary.

Thorpe clearly did not neglect the needs of his constituents, speaking effectively in the House and regularly meeting the voters at surgeries and other events in the towns and villages of North Devon. But unlike many MPs, he was absolutely confident that he could leave the day-to-day running of the constituency to the members of what was becoming a formidable team. The by-now well-oiled party machine, which had helped him almost halve the Tory majority in 1955 and then wipe it out completely four years later, was maintaining the momentum of the General Election campaigns, building up membership and expanding its ability to raise the funds necessary to match Conservative electoral spending.

Thorpe's youth and enthusiasm, coupled with his inherent belief in a brighter future for the party, helped him stand out from his fellow MPs and the party's national officials, whose only target in recent times had been sheer survival. He helped to found an unofficial campaign organisation within the party which became known as 'Winnable Seats' which, as the name suggests, envisaged directing the Liberals' scanty resources into identifying constituencies where there was a real chance of electoral success.

Previous policy had often been to fight as many Westminster seats as possible, in the hope of maintaining the perception among press and public that the Liberals were still a major national party, rather than the minority grouping that their Parliamentary representation revealed. The policy, as Thorpe clearly saw, led to lost deposits and a perception of failure that did nothing for party or voter morale.

The new approach led to some significant by-election performances in the period 1961-62, as the Conservatives and Macmillan began to lose some of the aura of invincibility that had surrounded the party and its leader in 1959. The climax of the Liberal revival in fortune had arrived in March 1962 at Orpington, in normally impregnable Tory territory. The candidate, Eric Lubbock, turned a Conservative majority of 14,760 into a Liberal majority of 7,855. Good results were also enjoyed in municipal elections and, briefly, national opinion polls showed the Liberals level-pegging with the Tories and Labour.

At the 1964 General Election, there were hopes that the momentum established in recent times could substantially boost the Liberals standing. The party did indeed almost double its share of the national vote, to more than eleven per cent, but given Britain's first past the post electoral system, this was only sufficient to give the Liberals a net gain of two seats (one being Bodmin, won by Peter Bessell).

The imbalance between electoral popularity and actual Parliamentary representation was, and still is, a major Liberal/Liberal Democrat bugbear. The question of changing to a system of proportional representation was in future to prove a major bargaining point whenever the two major parties required Liberal support and in 2010, when the Conservatives failed to gain an overall majority, a vote on the subject was one of the conditions insisted upon before the party, by then led by Nick Clegg, would agree to enter into a formal coalition.

The United Kingdom Alternative Vote referendum, was duly held on Thursday 5 May 2011, when a proposal to introduce AV was overwhelmingly rejected by 67.9%, of voters on a national turnout of 42%.

Following the '64 election and now seemingly safe on his home ground, Thorpe took steps to strengthen his national power base. His speeches, full of wit and wicked barbs against the other parties and their leaders, were a highlight of Liberal party assemblies. In 1965 he became the party's national treasurer and proved to be an effective fund raiser, despite his demand to exercise personal control of sections of funding which aroused resentment in some quarters.

One of Thorpe's interests since student days had been the developing world, Africa in particular, and the mid-1960s brought an opportunity for him to enhance his international reputation. In July 1965, following the ending of the Federation of Rhodesia and Nyasaland, Jeremy toured central and east Africa, including visits to Zambia and Rhodesia. Thorpe formed the opinion that the all-white Rhodesian government under its Prime Minister, Ian Smith, would make a unilateral declaration of independence, unless faced with armed intervention by British forces, and on his return to the UK briefed Prime Minister Harold Wilson along those lines. Wilson was not prepared to use force and the UDI Thorpe had forecast came about in November 1965.

Harold Wilson's Labour government could not survive for a full term on such a slim majority. The Premier called a General Election for March 1966, in the middle of the Swinging Sixties which ushered in a more radical flavour to British life, and was duly rewarded with a new majority of nearly 100 seats. Although the Liberal share of the national vote slipped to eight and a half percent, the party increased its number of MPs from nine to 12, fully justifying Thorpe's Winnable Seats idea. But politics is a fickle game, and in North Devon Jeremy's majority of more than 5,000 recorded in 1964 was cut heavily to just 1,166.

The Rhodesian UDI proved stubborn and in a speech to the Liberal Assembly in September 1966, Thorpe was highly critical of Wilson's handling of the Rhodesia crisis, calling it misjudged and misplanned, and called for the United Nations to bomb and destroy the rail link which delivered Rhodesia's oil supplies. The call split Liberal opinion; it outraged many Conservative MPs, who supported the Ian Smith regime, and their use of the nickname 'Bomber Thorpe' was soon being echoed by the Tory press.

The 1966 General Election was the third at which the Liberals had been led by Jo Grimond. Although a degree of respectability had been restored to the party in both Parliament and the country as a whole, it was not the breakthrough that many party members dreamed of. Grimond informed the party leadership of his intention to stand down and his formal resignation was received on 17 January 1967, with an election to find a new leader scheduled to take place within just 48 hours, making the behind the scenes lobbying and consultations, typical of the other political parties, a virtual impossibility.

Jeremy Thorpe's high public profile and obvious abilities had led to him being widely spoken of as Grimond's most likely successor, although Timothy (later Lord) Beaumont, who chaired the party's organising committee, had apparently noted in his diary that in his opinion Thorpe enjoyed 'little popularity' within the Parliamentary party. In the event, three candidates emerged. The issue was to be decided solely by the 12 Liberal MPs and when the votes were counted on the first ballot Jeremy Thorpe had six and his rivals, Eric Lubbock, the victor of Orpington and Emlyn Hooson, who represented Montgomeryshire, three each. Lubbock and Hooson withdraw from the contest and Thorpe was declared to be the winner.

Less than eight years after entering the House of Commons, Jeremy Thorpe achieved his ambition to lead the Liberal party. As others discovered before and after Thorpe it was no sinecure. The party was proud of its individuality and as the 1960s progressed, it increasingly provided an umbrella under which, perhaps to an even greater degree than was the case with the other political parties, people of widely divergent views found a convenient place to shelter, bicker and plot.

The Young Liberals, so useful to Thorpe in his own constituency, where any extreme radical tendencies were held firmly in check by the organisation's leadership, were to prove a thorn in the new leader's side in national terms. The policies being espoused by the leaders of the party's youth wing were far to the left of the Liberal mainstream, demanding withdrawal from NATO and extensive defence cuts, and suggesting workers' control in nationalised industries.

It was not as if the political climate of the time was in favour of radicalism; the Wilson government had enjoyed a relatively short honeymoon period after their 1966 General Election success. It was a time when there was a fad for car stickers proclaiming various messages, and the author remembers that a popular example seen in the rear windows of Austin 1100s and Vauxhall Vivas was *'Don't blame me – I voted Conservative'*. The Tories won several by-election victories during the period at the expense of Labour, and the Liberals were struggling again to make an impact on the political scene.

It was at this point that Jeremy Thorpe married Caroline Allpass, an art expert who worked in the Impressionists department at Sotheby's, the British-founded brokers of fine and decorative art, jewellery, real estate and collectible items, which now has headquarters in New York. She was the daughter of a furniture manufacturer from Surrey. The marriage took place at the end of May 1968, in the private chapel of Lambeth Palace, the official London residence of the Archbishop of Canterbury.

Those who had been fomenting discontent within the party chose to strike against the leader whilst he was on his honeymoon. Fortunately for Thorpe and the credibility of the Liberals, there was no real support for any move to ditch the leader and the plot was seen both by party activists and the public as treachery. When Thorpe returned the party executive backed him by 48 votes to 2.

Thorpe now enjoyed a period of stability, at least within his personal life, with a son, Rupert, being born in April 1969. This was followed by an unexpected boost for the leader, when the Liberals took a supposedly safe seat from increasingly unpopular Labour in the Birmingham Ladywood Constituency.

Despite this (sole) success, the party went into the 1970 General Election with no great confidence. The pessimism was justified; the share of the vote dropped to 7.5 per cent and seven of the party's thirteen seats (including the recently gained Ladywood) were lost. In North Devon Jeremy Thorpe's majority, badly dented in 1966, was reduced to 369 – just seven votes more than his first winning margin in 1959. Of the surviving Liberals, three of Thorpe's colleagues also had small majorities, with only Hooson in Wales and Grimond in the far north being safe. The Conservatives, led by Edward Heath, recorded a majority of 30 in the Commons.

When the smoke had cleared in the aftermath of the election, the knives began to come out again for Thorpe's leadership. As it was, criticism was stifled when, just ten days after polling, Caroline Thorpe was killed in a car crash. She was driving alone through Basingstoke, Hampshire, when her Ford Anglia estate car was in collision with a lorry at a roundabout on the A30 road. Caroline was alive when taken from the car and given oxygen in an ambulance but died shortly after arrival at Basingstoke General Hospital.

Jeremy Thorpe and Rupert, then 14 months old, had travelled to London by rail on the previous day after spending some time recovering from the strain of the recent General Election at the family cottage at Cobbaton. Thorpe wanted to be at the House of Commons for the election of the speaker and the news was broken to him at Westminster. Caroline Thorpe was carrying the family luggage in her car when the collision occurred.

Dr Michael Winstanley, who had been MP for Cheadle, Cheshire, paid a typical tribute, saying: "I did not know Caroline for long, but she was obviously the right sort of person to be with Jeremy at election time."

The political correspondent of the Conservative-supporting *Daily Telegraph* reflected the shock felt by MPs and the general public when he wrote: "News of his wife's death reached Mr Thorpe at the Commons soon after he had made a brief speech welcoming the re-election of Dr Horace King as Speaker. Overcome with grief, he left immediately. MPs of all parties were shocked to hear of his bereavement after only 25 months of ideally happy married life. It was bad enough, they felt, to see his party halved in the General Election (of 1970). To have his personal life shattered at the very moment the new

Parliament met was almost more than anyone could bear. Mrs Thorpe was a favourite with everyone. Her charm and friendliness made her the ideal political hostess and she quickly acquired a shrew judgement of affairs which must have been of great value to her husband."

In North Devon agent Lilian Prowse told reporters: "Caroline was a delightful woman. We all loved her." The last occasion on which Mrs Prowse had spoken to Caroline was just a few days before the crash. "She was full of plans for adapting the cottage in the constituency, which had been chosen because her ancestors had lived nearby, to the needs of her husband and son."

Assistant agent Peter Bray was a member of the then Barnstaple Borough Council at the time of the crash and vividly remembers how he was told the news of the accident. "I remember the then mayor, Guy Casey coming into the Guildhall in Barnstaple, looking straight at me and saying, 'I have some sad news, Caroline Thorpe has been killed in a car crash.'"

Peter was involved in the planning for the memorial to Caroline on Codden Hill, not far from the Thorpe's Cobbaton cottage and the highest point in the area, and was present at its dedication in 1971 by the then Archbishop of Canterbury, Michael Ramsay, and the Bishop of Crediton, Wilfred Westall. He recalls that one of Jeremy Thorpe's most endearing traits was his ability to talk naturally to ordinary people. "This obviously rubbed off on to a great many other important people on the occasions when they came into close contact with Jeremy. I was present at the dedication ceremony of the memorial, a stone pillar eleven and a half feet (3.5 metres) high, and a local coach driver, Claude Pugsley, managed to get his bus carrying the Archbishop, Bishop and other dignitaries close to the monument. When we boarded the bus Jeremy said, 'you sit there', and I realised I was next to the Archbishop, who spoke to me as if I was a long-lost friend."

For a longish period of time Jeremy Thorpe was pre-occupied with his shattering loss and his plan for a memorial for his wife. But if Harold Wilson had enjoyed just a brief honeymoon period in the aftermath of 1966, Heath's popularity was also to be short-lived and Liberal fortunes began to recover, largely in municipal elections where the party adopted 'community politics', concentrating on issues which to those preoccupied with the national scene seem minor, but which to local people across the nation were of great importance. The policy was at least partly developed on the streets of Barnstaple and North Devon under the aegis of Lilian Prowse and her helpers.

As the 1970s moved on Thorpe was able to see some of the political beliefs he had long held at heart actually come to fruition. He played an important role in helping through the Commons Heath's European Communities Bill, opening the way to UK membership of the European Economic Community, or Common Market. The bill had opponents in both the Conservative and Labour parties but by committing his MPs to the government side, Thorpe ensured its passage through the house and into law.

The roller-coaster ride of the Liberal party under Jeremy Thorpe's leadership now began to inch slowly up the incline once again. Both the Conservative government and the Labour opposition enjoyed little public confidence in

1972, community politics were proving popular and the Liberals enjoyed success in both local elections and in by-elections. On the Westminster front, the party won Rochdale from Labour and Sutton from the Conservatives and (in 1973) Isle of Ely, Ripon and Berwick on Tweed from the Conservatives.

Jeremy Thorpe's private life took an upward turn when, on 14 March 1973, he married Marion Stein, a concert pianist and the former wife of George Lascelles, 7th Earl of Harewood, a cousin of The Queen. The couple had been brought together a year earlier by a mutual acquaintance, the pianist Moura Lympany. In the years to come, right up to her death, Marion would maintain a fierce loyalty to her husband.

The Conservative administration elected in 1970 had been wracked by economic and industrial strife and in February 1974 Prime Minister Edward Heath decided to go to the country, essentially on a platform of who should run the country, the elected government or the trades unions. When the country went to the polls on 28 February Heath got the answer he least wanted or probably expected. When the votes were counted Britain had a hung Parliament; Labour had 301 seats and the Tories 297. Thorpe's Liberals made a big advance, winning eight additional seats for a total of 14, the highest Westminster representation the party had enjoyed for many years.

The sort of opportunity that Thorpe had long desired, with Liberals (almost) holding the balance of power, appeared to have arrived. Heath opted not to resign, the prerogative of a sitting Prime Minister in the prevailing circumstances. He hoped to persuade the Liberals to join a Conservative-led coalition and met Jeremy Thorpe on 2 March to discuss possible means of co-operation.

Discussions started and, for those who lived through the events, the gap between polling day on 28 February and the eventual settlement of the impasse seemed endless. Heath proposed a formal coalition in which Thorpe would receive a cabinet post and other senior Liberals would be allocated junior ministerial roles. As the combined Conservative/Liberal vote in the election had amounted to 57 per cent of the electorate, it was argued that such an arrangement would have considerable legitimacy. If the Liberals would not accept a full coalition, there would be a less formal basis of co-operation which would enable Heath to hang on to office.

Jeremy Thorpe, with the eyes of the nation and the TV cameras upon him, left Downing Street to confer with colleagues. Their response was predictable; the trade-off for a deal with Heath and the Conservatives would be electoral reform. The Liberals had for long complained bitterly (and continue to do so to this day) that the number of MPs they customarily elect does not reflect the size of their vote. Proportional representation, as practised in many European nations, rather than the British first past the post method, was a fairer system.

Heath could not make a firm commitment; his own party would never tolerate it. He was able to offer only a Speaker's Conference, to consider the whole issue of electoral reform and make recommendations which, if acceptable to the Liberals, would then be the basis of legislation with full cabinet approval. Heath hedged even on this modest offer, making it clear that while his MPs would not object to a Speaker's Conference, he could not commit them to voting in favour of any proposed legislation on a free House of Commons vote.

This time, it was the Liberals and Jeremy Thorpe who demurred. Thorpe's final shot was to offer the idea of an all-party Government of National Unity, to take in hand the urgent economic problems facing Britain. Heath preferred to resign on 4 March and Harold Wilson, who had been waiting patiently in the wings, formed a minority Labour government.

Thorpe later accepted that any coalition government would have torn the Liberals apart. The more radical members of the party, and in particular the Young Liberals, would never have accepted such an arrangement. In any case, even a fusion of Tories and Liberals would not have produced an administration with much of a life expectancy. The Ulster Unionists had withdrawn from acceptance of the Conservative whip over an issue concerning Northern Ireland and there were also the Scottish nationalists (with seven MPs) and the first Plaid Cymru (Welsh Nationalist) members to have been elected in a General Election rather than a by-election. Any coalition could have been brought down by the first vote following The Queen's Speech to open the new session of Parliament.

The waiting game at the beginning of March 1974 took the spotlight away from the very significant advance the Liberals had made at the General Election. Jeremy Thorpe's party had taken a considerable share of the popular vote from both Conservatives and Labour. But, highlighting why proportional representation had been THE issue during the inter-party discussions, the six million plus votes the Liberals had attracted at the polls – two and a half times the vote share achieved at the previous General Election in 1970 – had produced just 14 MPs.

It was an advance, but fell below media predictions that the party could elect many more members of Parliament.

In North Devon, Jeremy Thorpe achieved his best electoral result. In a constituency that now included (1973-84 only) the Borough of Bideford, the Urban District of Northam and the Rural District of Bideford, Thorpe amassed the massive total of 34,052 votes, 11,072 more than his closest opponent, Conservative Tim Keigwin. On the two previous occasions Keigwin had run Thorpe close – just 369 votes had separated the two men in 1970 – but faced with this huge majority Keigwin quit the race for good,

Harold Wilson's minority government had little chance of passing any meaningful legislation and he called a further General Election for October 1974. Jeremy Thorpe went into battle with high hopes, reportedly aiming first for a complete electoral breakthrough, with entering a coalition as a last resort. Although the party's slogan *'One More Heave'* was considered by some to be uninspiring, Thorpe was not short of innovative ideas.

A coalition might have been the last resort as far as Jeremy was concerned, but resorts of the seaside variety were at the forefront of his campaigning thoughts. The party, he decided, would hire a hovercraft and the leader and his acolytes would come up out of the sea and land on the beaches and slipways of Britain. The crowds certainly came out to meet the Liberal leader and colleagues who included John Pardoe, MP for North Cornwall and Paul Tyler of Bodmin.

Disaster struck at the genteel South Devon resort of Sidmouth, perhaps not particularly noted for the strength of its surf, when a huge wave submerged the hovercraft, threatening to drown Thorpe and the other occupants and rendering the machine inoperable. The press handout for one leg of the tour promised that the hovercraft would be carrying a heavyweight cargo when it arrived at Ilfracombe, Westward Ho!, Bude, Newquay and St Ives, in the shape of the later disgraced Rochdale MP Cyril Smith.

The results of the October '74 General Election , the third and final contest with Jeremy Thorpe as leader, did not meet his or the party's expectations. Harold Wilson won a narrow overall majority of three seats but the Liberals failed to advance on this occasion, actually losing one seat. In North Devon Thorpe's majority fell to 6,721, a blow but still a comfortable lead over a new Tory contender, Tony Speller, of whom North Devon would eventually hear a lot more.

On this occasion, there were no calls for Thorpe from Downing Street, as there had been eight months earlier. And in addition to political strain, Thorpe was increasingly under pressure from a man named Norman Scott.

5. Scott, Poll Defeat, Trial and a Pyrrhic Victory

One of the fascinating and still largely unanswered questions concerning the Norman Scott affair is the extent to which the circumstances surrounding the relationship between Jeremy Thorpe and his accuser were known to the MP's associates, both within the Liberal party nationally and in the North Devon constituency, and amongst his political opponents.

The likely answer is that, at an official level, through dossiers on Thorpe's private life compiled by the police and the security services, there was considerable awareness both in London and in Devon of his alleged homosexual activities and the potential risks being run by a man who, as the sixties and seventies ran their course, increasingly became a household name, at least among the politically conscious. When Norman Scott began to make allegations to the police and the Liberal party (which initially exonerated Thorpe), his claims were documented and, at least initially, filed away.

In North Devon, throughout the 1960s and early 1970s, few questions were being openly asked, although there was always the saloon bar gossip that surrounds any public figure, and particularly a flamboyant bachelor like Jeremy Thorpe. Malcolm Prowse, then a teenager at Barnstaple Boys' Grammar School, remembers the 'inevitable sneers and comments' but believes that ordinary voters in North Devon, continuing to relish the limelight the political activities of their MP focused on the area, had little real interest in his private life.

On the wider question of whether Liberal activists in the constituency were aware of anything that might be considered untoward, he points to the fact that little worth knowing escaped the notice of his mother, as constituency agent. "Both she and my father were very shrewd, but until Scott's allegations began to attract media attention, which was in the 1970s, nobody really took a great deal of notice.

"A great many people, both the party activists and the ordinary voters, were very loyal to Jeremy and were to remain so. The nonconformist voters in many instances just closed their ears to the allegations that were increasingly being made in the press. Obviously, at the 1979 General Election Jeremy was heavily defeated, but I tend to agree with those who believe that the chapel people, who formed a vital part of his electoral support, did not so much vote *against* Jeremy but rather turned their backs on the whole process and abstained."

It is generally accepted that Scott (then known as Norman Josiffe) first made the acquaintance of Jeremy Thorpe in 1961. At the time Scott was employed as a groom in stables owned by a friend of Thorpe. Almost twelve months after the first, brief meeting, Scott visited the House of Commons to ask the MP for help. Jeremy Thorpe acknowledged that a friendship then developed, but denied (right up to the point of his death) that any physical relationship had taken place.

Over the years Scott surfaced at intervals in Thorpe's life and alleged that the MP had seduced him. Although Thorpe attempted from time to time to help Scott find work and somewhere to live, Scott began to threaten the MP with exposure. Jeremy Thorpe involved his then friend and (from 1964) Parliamentary colleague Peter Bessell, Liberal MP for Bodmin. What happened next was to form the prosecution evidence in Thorpe's subsequent trial.

Jeremy Thorpe's election in 1967 as leader of the Liberals raised even higher his already significant national profile. At the same time it seemed to stoke the fire of Scott's ire and increase the risk that he would persist in his allegations. The risk level rose even further as the Liberals recovered their old confidence and verve under Thorpe's leadership, with the party achieving its highest level of post-war popularity at the February 1974 General Election, in the immediate aftermath of which Jeremy was involved in (ultimately abortive) talks with Conservative Prime Minister Edward Heath, who was attempting to cling on to office despite failing to gain an overall majority at the election.

Political commentator Dominic Sandbrook summed up the situation in a succinct sentence, writing: "The stakes had never been higher; silencing Scott had never been more urgent."

As the second half of the 1970s dawned a number of events began to intensify the pressure on Thorpe. October 1975 saw the incident in which the airline pilot Andrew Newton made the attempt to shoot Scott that resulted in the killing of Scott's dog, Rinka. And in the early months of 1976 two events caused this pressure to become virtually irresistible.

The first event, whilst unconnected with the Scott problem, nonetheless did little for Jeremy Thorpe's reputation. In January the Department of Trade published its report into the collapse of a company called London and County Securities, of which Thorpe had become a director. Commentators later suggested that his need for a financial boost to his relatively small Parliamentary income caused him to fail to take sufficient notice of warnings he received about the company's viability.

When in 1973 the firm collapsed, unveiling what the *Daily Telegraph* described as 'a tangled skein of financial misdemeanour', it was revealed that London and County Securities was charging 280 per cent interest on second mortgages. The matter was deeply embarrassing for Thorpe itself and the Liberal party, which had criticised the involvement of the Conservative minister Reginald Maudling in another recent financial scandal, the Poulson affair. Poulson was an architect and businessman whose use of bribery was disclosed in 1972. Maudling, as Home Secretary in the Heath government, was the highest-ranking figure to be damaged by the affair.

The Department of Trade's report into the London and County Securities affair was critical of Jeremy Thorpe's failure to investigate the true nature of the company before becoming involved in its affairs.

The second event to raise the stakes for Thorpe came in March 1976, when

Andrew Newton was tried on charges of possession of a firearm with intent to endanger life, arising out of the incident with Norman Scott's dog Rinka. The trial gave Norman Scott another platform for repeating his allegations against the Liberal leader. Newton was found guilty and given two years in prison, but said nothing during the proceedings to incriminate Thorpe.

March continued to bring problems for the Liberals, with the party recording poor results in by-elections during the month, leading some party figures to blame a loss of confidence in Thorpe as leader. Thorpe responded to Scott's allegations, described as lies, in an article in the *Sunday Times*. The media, which had been hesitant until this point, now began to smell blood and the situation was not improved by a media 'confession' by Peter Bessell that in his earlier statements he had lied to protect his former leader.

On 10 May 1976 Jeremy Thorpe resigned the leadership of the Liberal party, being quoted as saying that he was "convinced that a fixed determination to destroy the leader could itself result in the destruction of the party."

At this stage there was still hope for Thorpe that he could continue to be a significant political player. The new Liberal leader, David Steel, made Jeremy the party spokesman on foreign affairs, with responsibility for European issues. In March 1977 Labour Prime Minister James Callaghan, who had succeeded Harold Wilson after the latter's resignation, lost his majority and entered into a pact with the Liberals in Parliament, who agreed to support the government on confidence issues. Thorpe played a part in the negotiations which led to the pact, insisting that one of the conditions for Liberal support should be legislation for direct elections to the European Parliament; he failed however in his principal objective, a commitment to proportional representation in these elections.

Despite this temporary lull following his resignation as leader, the media was working behind the scenes on investigations into the Scott affair. This reached the headlines again in October 1977, when Andrew Newton was released from prison and sold his story to the London *Evening News*, claiming that he had been paid 'by a leading Liberal' to kill Scott.

Jeremy Thorpe's attempts to continue with a normal Parliamentary career were by this stage proving to be impossible, and the situation reached a climax in early August '77. He made what would prove to be his final speech in the House of Commons on 2 August, during a debate on Rhodesia – the fate of Britain's former colonial possessions remained an abiding interest, with Thorpe pressing for the involvement of representatives from the African nationalists, in the form of the Patriotic Front, in negotiations for a peaceful settlement to the long-running bush war in the country.

Then, on 4 August, Jeremy's Parliamentary life came to an abrupt end, when he was formally charged with incitement to murder. Released on bail, he remained the Member of Parliament for North Devon but effectively withdrew into a state of limbo as far as public life was concerned.

Committal for trial proceedings were held in November 1978 at Minehead, the Somerset seaside resort close to the scene of the shooting of Norman Scott's dog, on Porlock Hill, Exmoor. Evidence of a conspiracy was heard by the local magistrates from Norman Scott, Andrew Newton and Peter Bessell; Thorpe and his fellow defendants, his friend David Holmes, John le Mesurier (a carpet salesman and not the star of *Dad's Army)*, and George Deakin, were committed for trial at The Old Bailey.

The trial was set to begin on 30 April 1979 but the situation was complicated by the announcement of a General Election for 3 May 1979. The background to the contest was the struggle Labour, under first Harold Wilson and then his successor as Prime Minister, Jim Callaghan, had faced ever since taking office as a minority government in October 1974. Against a background of grave economic problems and rising trade union militancy Labour had managed to govern with the assistance of the Liberals, for much of the time under the Lib-Lab Pact, a formal arrangement which lasted from 1977 to 1978.

When the Lib-Lab pact collapsed Callaghan eventually lost a no confidence motion in the House of Commons and had no choice but to go to the country. For North Devon and the Liberal party, the proximity of the Thorpe trial and the election posed a dilemma. If the trial could be delayed until after voting had taken place, would it be right in the circumstances for Jeremy Thorpe to stand for re-election, under the shadow of what have been described as the most serious criminal charges ever brought against a British politician (at least in the modern era)?

Opinions varied within the Liberal party, both nationally and in North Devon, both on the issue of a Thorpe candidacy and on the question of whether or not the trial should be postponed. Thorpe's solicitor, Sir David Napley, said that in the event of the North Devon Constituency Association inviting Jeremy to stand, and if he agreed to do so, an application for a postponement would be made to the trial judge. Napley doubted whether the prosecution in the case would attempt to oppose a postponement.

The Liberals nationally and locally were well aware of the dangers of seeming to support special treatment for Jeremy Thorpe as a politician and public figure. One national newspaper had speculated that Jeremy's successor as leader, David Steel, might call for a fresh date for the trial 'with an eye on the Parliamentary scene that could spell a crucial no confidence vote'. Steel hit back, saying he was 'astonished' by the newspaper report, adding that the party believed 'justice must be done.'

Speaking for the North Devon party, Peter Bray said the local association had not asked for a postponement, adding: "Justice must not only be done, it must be seen to be done."

In a twist to the story, the London *Evening Standard* suggested in March of '79 that 'the front runner to succeed Thorpe on the local Liberal party's list of possibles is still Marion Thorpe'. Peter Bray, standing in as agent at the time for the unwell Lilian Prowse, was diplomatic in his response to the story, which appeared in the *Standard's* gossip column, *Londoner's Diary*, saying: "Obviously her (Marion's) name has been suggested but that does not mean by us. We are going to have meetings in the next few days and the subject of our candidate will obviously be the most urgent matter in hand."

In the event, there was to be no new candidate. Jeremy Thorpe was determined to stand and believed, no doubt correctly, that stepping down from the candidacy would be seen as an admission of guilt. The trial was duly postponed and the election campaigning began, in unprecedented circumstances, and with no-one really knowing what to expect. Jeremy Thorpe's Conservative opponent was once again to be Tony Speller, who in October 1974 had reduced Thorpe's record majority of 11,000 plus, recorded in February of that year, to fewer than 7,000 votes.

Speller had held on to the candidacy for the four years and seven months that the Labour government survived. Both the Conservative candidate and his party approached the forthcoming contest with mixed feelings. The circumstances appeared to give Speller a much improved chance of victory. On the other hand, the Conservative candidate and his party needed to walk on eggshells to avoid accusations of exploiting the accusations against a man not yet tried for his alleged offences (and who was subsequently to be acquitted of all charges against him).

The campaign was described at the time by one political commentator as being 'surreal'. In addition to the main players in the drama, Thorpe and Speller, there was not only the customary Labour contender but also a raft of minor candidates, some serious players but others clearly involved simply to take advantage of the huge amount of media coverage the campaign would inevitably attract to cause the maximum mischief.

The 1970s had seen a gradual growth in the number of candidates standing for Parliament, especially at high-profile by-elections and in constituencies where the sitting MP or candidate was a well-known political figure. When the date for nominations for North Devon closed it was revealed that the ballot paper would contain a total of nine names. Thorpe and Speller were to be joined in battle by Labour's Antony Saltern, Tony Whittaker of the Ecology Party (a forerunner of the Greens), Frank Hansford-Miller of the English National Party, who had stood against Thorpe in October 1974, and John Morley-Price of the extreme right wing National Front.

In addition, the list included Henrietta Elizabeth Rous, a member of a noted Liberal family, standing as a Wessex Regionalist, Bill Boaks, campaigning as a Democratic Monarchist Public Safety White Resident, and, perhaps most exotic of all, Auberon Waugh, the writer and a noted contributor to *Private Eye* magazine, which had to date taken a considerable interest in the Norman Scott affair.

Waugh, the son of the novelist Evelyn Waugh, of *Brideshead Revisited* fame, represented his own Dog Lover's Party, in an obvious allusion to the shooting of Scott's dog, Rinka.

As campaigning began the North Devon Liberals were, not surprisingly, concerned that their Conservative opponents should try to exploit the circumstances. And there were fears, which turned out to be justified to a significant extent, that the traditional link between North Devon nonconformist religion and the Liberal cause would be shattered by the pre-trial 'revelations' in the press about the Scott affair and would turn Methodist and Baptist voters against Thorpe.

Alec Pickersgill, now retired and living in Bideford, was the agent for the

Conservatives in North Devon in 1979. The local association, and Conservative Central Office, had decreed that there should be no mention of the peculiar circumstances in which the poll was being held. The Liberals, determined that this unofficial pact of silence should be observed to the letter, monitored Conservative election meetings.

Pickersgill recalls: "It was said that a representative of the Liberals attended all of Tony Speller's meetings, to make notes of anything he said about the Scott affair. But as a professional agent with wide experience, I would not have been a party to anything of that sort. One of the first rules of fighting an election is to never ever mention your opponent. Having said that, no-one could control what was being talked about in Barnstaple and the surrounding villages. The inevitable jokes in pubs, in my opinion, helped to shatter the image of Jeremy Thorpe to a substantial degree."

Jeremy Thorpe was greeted by 'scenes of euphoria' and a standing ovation when he walked into his adoption meeting at the North Devon Motel. Ominously, he was accompanied by a bevy of TV and film cameramen. Press representatives were packed tight around the platform when Thorpe began to speak. He warned the media pack that there were matters to be resolved after the election which it would be "improper for me – and I may say improper for the press – to discuss during the campaign", adding: "Suffice it to say that I have vigorously asserted my innocence and am determined to establish it at the appropriate time."

The meeting heard a recorded message from David Steel, who said that 'whatever problems you have all had in the past months are irrelevant to the battle on which you are now embarking.'

Throughout the 1979 campaign Jeremy Thorpe maintained his dignity despite events which at times deteriorated into farce. It was Tony Speller who hit out at the activities of some of the minor candidates, saying: "We are being treated as some kind of funny farm and I am sick of it." Speller added: "I bear no candidate ill-will because to offer oneself for public office is an honourable activity, and personal abuse is inappropriate. Nevertheless I fail to see why North Devonians should submit to the personal publicity activities of eccentric candidates; North Devon deserves better."

Speller was particularly harsh in his dismissal of the National Front man, saying: "Racialism has no future in North Devon. I detest the fake patriotism of those who wave the union jack in front of people's faces to disguise the Nazi salute behind it."

There was an initial clash between the two main candidates when Speller rejected a suggestion that a Conservative government would remove the Development Area status which Jeremy Thorpe had fought so hard to obtain for North Devon (and which in 2018 is still regarded as one of his finest achievements for the constituency). Any ill-feeling appeared to have been forgotten when the two men met later in Barnstaple cattle market, shaking hands and exchanging some banter before going their separate ways.

Jeremy Thorpe and the Liberals, whilst not expecting an easy ride, appear to have had a degree of confidence at least that the size of their majority would act as a buffer against defeat by his Tory opponent. Thorpe himself told the media: "I never count my chickens before they are hatched. Over 20 years, my majorities have always been either much bigger or much smaller than I thought. But we had a large majority last time and I simply don't see that dissipating sufficiently for them to win the seat." Another reason for confidence, he added, was the 'heartening support' he had experienced at his village meetings.

Derek Henderson, the experienced *North Devon Journal Herald* journalist, attended the count at the Queen's Hall, Barnstaple after polling had finished on 3 May. He told readers that Jeremy Thorpe had known for some time before the announcement of the result that he had lost his seat in Parliament. The neatly stacked piles of voting papers, obviously far more for the Conservatives than for Thorpe, gave the game away.

The sheer size of the Tory majority – Speller turned a deficit of 6,700 at the October '74 contest into a majority of 8,473 – took away the breath of the Conservative supporters and left the Liberals devastated. All through the proceedings, and especially when defeat was obvious, Thorpe masked his inner feelings with a control that Henderson described as 'little short of miraculous', adding: "With an expressionless face (Thorpe) listened to the official result."

Tony Speller, who shook hands with Thorpe and patted his opponent on the back as the former Liberal leader left the room, appeared to be acutely conscious of the fact that his thumping victory owed as much to the unfortunate circumstances as it did to his campaigning and the fact that the tide was running strongly in favour of the Conservatives and swamping what was seen as a failed Labour government in thrall to trade union extremism.

He paid a handsome tribute to his defeated opponent, saying that Jeremy Thorpe had been 'without equal as a constituency member' and later astutely summed up the situation in his maiden speech in the House of Commons, lamenting that "everyone knows who lost, but no one remembers yet who won."

The Labour representative and the minor party candidates were forgotten in the acclaim for the victor and the sympathy for the loser. Saltern for Labour polled a highly respectable 7,108 votes; the others managed just 1,257 votes between them. Boaks was bottom of the list with just 20 votes. Waugh did a little better, He had been quoted in the press during the campaign as saying that he would not campaign in the constituency as it would be 'a waste of time'. As he recorded just 79 votes the majority of the electorate clearly agreed with him.

What of the much vaunted nonconformist factor in the election? Several North Devon Liberals active at the time who were also committed members of their individual churches recall the circumstances very well and, like Malcolm Prowse, believe that many nonconformist voters, stunned by the allegations against their MP, did not so much turn against him as turn away from the contest altogether, staying at home on polling day.

David Worden was in 1979 chairman of the Young Liberals in both

Barnstaple and Devon and Cornwall as a whole, and a Methodist lay-preacher, who is still active today both in local government and church circles. He recalls canvassing in the run-up to the 1979 poll and says: "I was not particularly conscious of any hostility over the forthcoming trial. But what I was aware of was a reduced sense of commitment among voters. People who would in the past have been enthusiastic about voting for Jeremy were simply not committing themselves."

There is no doubt that the allegations against Thorpe hit many Liberal activists in North Devon hard, and particularly those whose Liberalism stemmed from nonconformist roots. Their essential loyalty to Jeremy never wavered, despite the taunts of hypocrisy directed at them from those who were not active Christians, but their enthusiasm in many cases was adversely affected by the affair.

Dairy farmer Gerald Waldon from Little Deptford, Chittlehampton, is proud of the fact that his work for the Liberal cause in North Devon pre-dates his ability to cast a vote. He says: "I was just 17 in 1959 when Jeremy Thorpe first won the seat and at that time of course you had to be 21 to vote. During the election campaign I spent a lot of time driving around with a friend getting the vote out, persuading people known or thought to be Liberals to go along to the polling stations, and in many cases actually taking them there."

As the years passed Gerald and his wife Daisy – Miss Chittlehampton Liberal 1964 – progressed from working with the Young Liberals to playing active roles in the local branch of the North Devon Association – one of the strongest village groups in an impressive network of around 50 local branches that, at their peak, covered the widespread constituency. Gerald was successively vice-chairman and then chairman of Chittlehampton Liberals and was also a member of the constituency consultative committee, the party's local powerhouse.

At the same time as his work for the Liberal party, Gerald Waldon was an active member of the Methodist Church, a lay preacher, and a circuit steward within the South Molton circuit. He remembers well the atmosphere of the 1979 election campaign "Despite the fact that he was eventually acquitted, for many people Jeremy Thorpe was found guilty right from the start of all the rumours and speculation, well before the trial, with not just the general public but, in my experience some of his nonconformist supporters taking that view.

"There was an eve of poll election meeting in Barnstaple Pannier Market, which featured all the candidates. I remember walking in as part of the group with Jeremy, all wearing our rosettes, and noticing a group of Methodists and they gave us dirty looks. I believed then and still believe that I am not in a position to judge another person's behaviour. I have enough to do coping with my own sins."

Gerald Waldon does admit to having perhaps held back a little from political affairs in the years that followed the 1979 election and the revelations of the Norman Scott affair, during which time he was often challenged to explain how someone with such a strong commitment to the Methodist Church and the morality it taught could tolerate the alleged behaviour revealed in the press and at the trial.

He nevertheless did not waver from his support for the Liberal party – "I know where my heart is", and retains to this day his admiration for Jeremy Thorpe as a constituency MP. "He achieved a great deal for North Devon, particularly where the hospital and the granting of assisted area status were concerned. He understood the area and its people."

Another farmer and Liberal activist from a nonconformist background, Albert Cook, who served the area as a councillor for more than 60 years, is still critical of what he believes was the lack of support given to Jeremy Thorpe by the party's national leadership. He says: "I believe David Steel, who had succeeded Thorpe as leader, and others at the top tried to disengage themselves. I became disenchanted with the party for forsaking Jeremy and after that election I never canvassed again, although I remained a Liberal supporter."

Albert Cook considers Thorpe to be "the epitome of a first class constituency MP – he did so much for North Devon. He was probably the best debater in the House of Commons and a real thorn in the side of the Tories, who were desperate to get rid of him."

Tony Speller went on to represent North Devon for 13 years, twice fighting off Liberal attempts to recapture the seat, and proved himself a conscientious constituency MP. He never held ministerial office, though Margaret Thatcher reportedly considered appointing him her Parliamentary Private Secretary. When, in 1991, American aircraft from Britain bombed Saddam Hussein's Iraq, Speller condemned 'lunatic' advice to B52 pilots that they should offload their unused bombs off the North Devon coast. He chaired the West Country MPs, the all-party alternative energy group and the Parliamentary West Africa Committee, and served on the Energy Select Committee. He died in 2013.

And so when the smoke cleared from the General Election the media circus moved on to the Old Bailey. Losing the seat he had held for 20 years was hardly the best preparation for Thorpe for the forthcoming proceedings in the austere surroundings of Britain's most famous criminal court.

The trial, which was to last for six weeks, began on 8 May 1979, before Mr Justice Cantley. Thorpe was defended by George Carman who destroyed much of the credibility of the key witness for the prosecution, Peter Bessell, by revealing that Bessell had a significant financial interest in Thorpe's conviction; should the former Liberal leader be acquitted, said Carmen, Bessell would receive only half of the agreed fee for selling his story to a newspaper.

When Carman cross-examined Norman Scott he asked: "You knew Thorpe to be a man of homosexual tendencies in 1961? This question has been represented as a stratagem to discourage the prosecution from calling witnesses who were prepared to testify as to Jeremy Thorpe's sex life. Despite this, Carman insisted, there was no reliable evidence of any physical sexual relationship between Thorpe and Scott, whom Carman dismissed as an 'inveterate liar, social climber and scrounger'.

The case for the defence opened on 7 June. Only one of the four defendants, George Deakin, testified. He told the court that although he had introduced Newton to Holmes, he had thought this was to help deal with a blackmailer.

He said that he knew nothing of a conspiracy to kill. Thorpe, le Mesurier and Holmes declined to testify on the grounds that the testimonies of Bessell, Scott and Newton had failed to make the case for the prosecution.

When Mr Justice Cantley began his summing up he emphasised Jeremy Thorpe's distinguished public record; by contrast he was scathing about the principal prosecution witnesses. Peter Bessell was dismissed as a 'humbug', Scott as 'a fraud, a sponger, a whiner and a parasite,' whilst Newton was 'determined to milk the case as hard as he can'. On 20 June the jury retired. The members returned two days later and acquitted the four defendants on all charges.

In the immediate aftermath of his acquittal, Jeremy Thorpe was understandably jubilant. The horrendous prospect of a long-term return to the sort of 'flea-ridden cell' where he had been held during the course of his trial no longer loomed. Images of the former Liberal leader captured on his emergence from the Old Bailey following the verdict of not guilty capture the whooping, fist-clenching joy of a fastidious man from whom the prospect of a significant term of imprisonment, with all its humiliations and privations, had been lifted. For a brief time at least his legendary exuberance had returned.

The euphoria was short-lived. In one of the most telling scenes in the 2018 television dramatisation of the affair, as Thorpe celebrates on the balcony of his London home, bottle of champagne in hand, his mother Ursula, in a whispered aside, tells him: "you do realise you are finished, don't you". Whether the scene and her comment actually occurred, or was a scriptwriter's later embellishment, matters little. For it *was* truly the end of his political career.

Jeremy Thorpe was a free man, but in his case the cliché 'an acquittal is not a certificate of innocence', was to cling to him until his death. If, as has been claimed, the establishment from the Prime Minister downwards had conspired to keep Thorpe out of prison, the trade-off on which they insisted was that the former Liberal leader had to accept that there was no future role for him in any significant area of public life.

Defence barrister George Carman's advice to Thorpe to invoke his right to silence and stay out of the witness box may have been a crucial factor in securing the acquittal, together with Carman's forensic shredding of the reputations of key prosecution witnesses, notably Peter Bessell and Norman Scott himself. But Thorpe's failure to explain himself under oath was widely criticised in the press, and the public perception was that he had been fortunate to have 'got off'.

Whether in the immediate aftermath of the trial Thorpe himself fully accepted that his reputation had suffered irretrievable damage, at least as far as the movers and shakers within the political world, including those with the power within his own party, may be debateable. What is certain is that many of his most ardent supporters in North Devon refused to believe that his active life was at an end.

To a not insignificant number of Liberal activists, and to many of those who had voted repeatedly for Jeremy over 20 years, the acquittal meant that his return to politics in the constituency was almost an expectation. They were determined to show their loyalty towards and their affection for their former

MP in the grand style which had become a hallmark of Jeremy Thorpe's tenure of the North Devon seat.

The people of the constituency picked up their copies of the Barnstaple-based *Journal Herald* newspaper on the Thursday following the court verdict to read the headline, 'Thorpe returns to Devon – Jubilant Jeremy back on Saturday'. Thorpe and Marion were, said the story, 'assured of a rapturous reception from fellow Liberals' when they appeared before a gathering at the Queen's Hall, Barnstaple, the scene of many of Jeremy's past triumphs.

Senior Liberals in the constituency were somewhat more circumspect than the newspaper's headline writers. Party organisers, no doubt influenced by the wisdom and experience of Lilian Prowse, were concerned that the event might seem too much like triumphalism. They went to considerable lengths to make it clear that the gathering was not so much a triumphant return as a 'routine thank you' to supporters for their loyalty at the general election – despite the crushing defeat more than 23,000 voters had stuck with Thorpe. Jeremy himself emphasised that the Queen's Hall event would be a private get-together with party workers and helpers. No invitations were to be sent to the press, allowing him to 'maintain a dignified silence to the world at large'.

The morning after the Queen's Hall gathering brought an even more contentious happening in the form of a Thanksgiving Service at St Peter's church in Bratton Fleming, a village on the fringe of Exmoor National Park. The service was organised by the Rector, the Rev. John Hornby, who was well known in North Devon as an ardent Liberal activist.

Once upon a time the Church of England was regarded as the Conservative party at prayer. That perception declined considerably during the second half of the twentieth century as the Anglican Church's social conscience became more prominent. A drift to the left of centre within the Church meant that Conservative Prime Minister Margaret Thatcher, who moved into 10 Downing Street in the wake of Thorpe's 1979 defeat, had some memorable spats with church leaders during her time in office.

The trend has continued; in the late summer of 2018 the current Archbishop of Canterbury, Justin Welby, co-authored a controversial research document, *Prosperity and Justice*, which argued that Britain's economy was not working for millions of people and needed fundamental reform.

John Hornby, then in his mid-fifties, had never been reticent about his political sympathies and he claimed to have been a Liberal activist in various parts of Britain for more than 20 years. Bratton Fleming was one of the many villages in the constituency to have its own Liberal association, which was chaired by the Rector. Mr Hornby was also a member of the North Devon Liberal Association consultative committee (known as 'the cabinet') and served on a small committee which assisted Peter Bray with publicity.

He made available a room at the Rectory for Liberal meetings and for use as a committee room at elections, and wrote long letters to the press denouncing the Conservative and Labour parties and urging a Liberal/Social Democratic majority in the House of Commons as being the most representative of all classes of society.

The media may not have been directly invited to the rally in Barnstaple the previous evening but they turned out in some force for the Thanksgiving Service, although contemporary reports which speak of the press outnumbering the actual congregation are exaggerated. The local media recorded a congregation of 90, with up to 20 considered to be journalists. In addition to Jeremy, Marion and Rupert Thorpe, friends who were sticking by the politician, including the Liberal MP for the Isle of Ely, Clement Freud, attended the service.

Many of the media people present were probably attracted to the service by a hoax allegedly perpetrated by staff and contributors to *Private Eye* magazine. A telephone call told the Rector that a coach party of gay activists would attend the service and the claim was leaked to the media, causing a small stampede of national media reporters and photographers to Bratton Fleming. On the day, no gay activists were to be seen or heard.

Mr Hornby was not dismayed by the smaller than expected turnout of genuine worshippers. He told those present: "We have the opportunity to give thanks to God for the ministry of his servant Jeremy in North Devon. In the long dark days of the committal proceedings at Minehead, and at the Old Bailey, God granted Marion and Jeremy that fantastic resilience which has aroused the admiration of the world. The darkness is now past and the true light shines. This is the day the Lord hath made. Now is the day of our salvation. Thanks be to God, for with God, nothing is impossible."

Not all of Mr Hornby's parishioners agreed with his up-front political stance or his idea for a Thanksgiving Service, and his immediate superior in the Church of England, the Archdeacon of Barnstaple, the Venerable Ronald Herniman, had doubts about the wisdom of the service and others within the Church of England felt it should have been a private, family occasion.

Feelings in the parish itself came to a head two years after the service, following a long letter the Rector wrote to the press attacking the Thatcher government and seeking to justify his own stance.

It was claimed that several members of Bratton Fleming's Parochial Church Council had resigned in protest at the Rector's political stance and what were described as his 'anti-Tory tirades' in the press. A former Church Council member, Lionel Bale, was quoted as saying: "He's quite entitled to his views but the position he holds does not warrant him spouting them all over the place. That's my view and that of several others."

The Archdeacon admitted that he had received complaints by letter, telephone and in conversation about the things Mr Hornby said, but defended the Rector's right to be politically active. Mr Horniman said: "It is true to say that his comments in the press are making Tories angry and Liberals very embarrassed. Every clergyman is entitled to hold political views and there is no reason why he should be politically illiterate. Where a clergyman acts within the law nothing can be done, unless there is a formal complaint from the church warden. As yet, no complaint has been received."

Mr Hornby fiercely denied that PCC members had resigned because of his politics and said church congregations had risen in recent times, with collections at services rising steeply. The Church Council itself issued a statement refuting what its members described as 'untrue allegations in the press'. The statement said: "The Rector's ministry of the word and sacraments is widely and deeply appreciated. We have every confidence in him." Finally, Liberal agent Peter Bray denied that the local party was embarrassed.

After the Barnstaple rally and the church service, Jeremy, Marion and Rupert Thorpe began the demanding task of continuing with their lives. On a personal note, a great deal of success was undoubtedly achieved, but for the politician who had been at the heart of Westminster life for two decades, there was to be mainly frustration.

Immediately after the trial, Thorpe had announced that he proposed to attend the 1979 Liberal Assembly and the forthcoming Liberal International Congress in Canada although, in the event, he stayed at home during both events.

As the weeks passed, Jeremy appeared to increasingly accept that there was no future role for him within the Liberal Party. He informed the North Devon Association that he would not seek to fight the seat again, and a new candidate, Roger Blackmore, was selected. New party leader David Steel, in merely expressing the hope that Thorpe 'after a suitable period of rest and recuperation', would find many avenues where his great talents may be used, was perhaps less than encouraging.

After the initial public outpourings of support and sympathy for Thorpe, exemplified by the Queen's Hall event in 1979 had subsided, the North Devon Liberal Association simply got on with life without the man who had dominated the constituency for 20 years.

Lilian Prowse retired from the post of full-time agent in August 1980, after a total of 24 years in office, the last six months of which had been spent supporting Roger Blackmore, the man the association had chosen as Thorpe's successor as parliamentary candidate. She told the *North Devon Journal Herald* that she felt the Liberal organisation in the constituency was 'strong and in such good spirits that I feel that this is a good time for me to begin to enjoy more leisure."

The *Journal Herald* paid fulsome tribute to Mrs Prowse, who had masterminded seven General Election campaigns for North Devon Liberals, and had during the years when Jeremy Thorpe led the party become a vitally important contact for national newspaper journalists and their overseas counterparts. The paper said that, while Mrs Prowse's public life was inexorably bound up with that of Mr Thorpe and his colourful career, she was a personality and character in her own right, adding: "And much of the credit for his election successes was put down to her efficient and painstaking organisational ability."

The local association was fortunate in having a man with a strong claim to Lilian Prowse's job – Roger Bray, who had been her assistant agent for nine years and prior to that had been agent for the Liberals in several by-elections in other parts of the country.

The new prospective candidate for North Devon, Roger Blackmore, 29 in 1980, was a Parliamentary candidate on no fewer than six occasions, without gaining a seat. Although based in Leicestershire, where he was a lecturer, he had strong North Devon connections with Swimbridge and had been educated at Shebbear College. His local government career was much more successful, and during the Liberal revival of the late twentieth century, he was leader of Leicester City Council from 2003 to 2004, leading a Liberal/Conservative coalition, and again from 2005 to 2007, and Lord Mayor of the city in 2009/10.

Roger Blackmore's task in North Devon was far greater than that which would have faced a new candidate replacing a former MP whose tenure of the seat had ended in more conventional circumstances. He had to follow a charismatic and popular politician, still regarded by many activists and electors as the 'king over the water', waiting in the wings to regain his throne when the time was right.

There is some evidence that Blackmore was valued more highly in the Liberal party as a whole than he was in North Devon. In June 1981 he was appointed as a member of the party's environment panel and it was reported that he was expected to play a key role in drawing up key policies on energy conservation and other environmental issues – an area which the Liberals recognised as increasingly important, some time before the other parties got on board.

Blackmore said: "It really is high time we got across our policies for the conservation of scarce resources, waste recycling, energy conservation and the control of pollution rather more forcibly. Liberals have so much in the way of positive policies to offer, in contrast to the old parties with their roots deep in economic self-interest."

But despite the brave words from Lilian Prowse and others, the wind *had* been taken out of the sails of the North Devon Liberals by the Scott affair and the Old Bailey trial. There is no denying the adverse effect upon voting intention with the Thorpe charisma missing. Added to that loss, Blackmore's one and only stab at regaining the seat for the Liberals (in 1983) came when the incumbent Conservative Prime Minister Margaret Thatcher, whose popularity had been on the wane, reaped the benefit of the successful military campaign to regain the Falkland Islands.

When the country went to the polls in '83, Blackmore was unable to reduce Tony Speller's 1997 majority, although the North Devon swing to the Conservatives, a mere +1.6, was smaller than the national swing. Despite this respectable showing, Blackmore was quickly replaced, but did not give in without a fight. He left North Devon after putting his personal case for being retained to the constituency party, together with his outline proposals for restructuring the organisation's political organisation.

In a statement he admitted that he had failed to gain the required two thirds majority, but added: "I was not dissatisfied by the vote I did secure; this is the full and open democratic process of which our party is truly proud. All members will be able to vote and have a real and effective voice in decision making."

The fact that there was again a vacancy for a prospective Liberal Parliamentary candidate in North Devon almost inevitably encouraged Jeremy

Thorpe's supporters to open a campaign for the return of the former MP. The campaign was well publicised by the local media, with a headline in the *Western Morning News* proclaiming *Liberals Hope for Thorpe Return*, whilst the Exeter *Express and Echo* led the front page with a story headed *Thorpe May Come Back*. The two stories revealed that after nearly four years out in the cold, with the job of Prospective Parliamentary Candidate for North Devon once more up for grabs, speculators and party pundits were again pointing at Jeremy Thorpe." The article accepted that Thorpe himself had insisted that he was 'unlikely' to apply for the position but commentators seized upon the word 'unlikely', which they claimed left the door open. There was, they said, 'a giant void in the public's imagination, which was being filled by speculation.'

It was undoubtedly accurate to suggest that there was a hard and vocal core of Liberal stalwarts in North Devon who would be delighted to welcome Thorpe back into the fold. But the story showed some political nous at least, by commenting that 'those supporters who flock around Jeremy Thorpe at coffee mornings, apparently entranced by his undoubted charisma, are the old faithful, not the decision makers'.

Thorpe's supporters believed it would take 'a special man' to wrest North Devon back from the Tories and they had no doubts as to who that man was. The campaign, nevertheless, was largely media-inspired and it is fair to say that neither Jeremy Thorpe himself, who recognised the realities of the situation, or the senior people within the constituency Liberal association, were behind it.

In place of Blackmore, a new prospective candidate was selected in June 1984, with a view to fighting the next General Election (eventually to be held three years later). He was David Short, described by the local press as a man who gave the impression that he had the physical and moral fibre to win North Devon back for the Liberals or, in the context of the times, the Alliance of Liberals and the Social Democratic Party (SDP).

Like Blackmore in the Midlands, Short was a leading figure in municipal politics in his home town of Hereford, serving as a city councillor and mayor and also as a county councillor. A devout Christian, he eventually became a Methodist minister, once again emphasising the traditional links between Liberalism and nonconformism.

The journalist who interviewed Short to introduce him to the North Devon public was obviously favourably impressed, describing the new man as 'chunky, full of drive, amiable and able to get along with people instantly'. Short never got the chance to put his qualities to the supreme test of acceptance by the North Devon electorate, disappearing from the scene before the 1987 election was called.

As it was, the 1987 General Election was to be contested by another Liberal stalwart, Michael Pinney, often referred to by another of his first names, Aza. He failed to win the seat, but reduced Conservative Tony Speller's 1983 majority from 8,727 to 4,469. It was not enough for North Devon; the Liberal Association had become accustomed to success during the Thorpe years. It would be another five years before Nick Harvey succeeded in ousting the

Conservatives, with a majority of fewer than 800 votes. It was the beginning of a run of success that exceeded even the Thorpe years, with Harvey in Parliament for 23 years, until defeated in 2015 by the Tory Peter Heaton-Jones, who was successful again in 2015 and 2017, on both occasions in a contest with the persistent Harvey.

Away from the political arena in the wider world, Jeremy Thorpe's search for those avenues of opportunity mentioned by David Steel had duly begun, although the initial signs were not encouraging. Attempts to resuscitate his once successful career in television led to nothing. Applications for the posts of administrator of the Aldeburgh Festival and as race relations adviser to the Greater London Council were unsuccessful.

Both jobs were worthy, but were hardly comparable to the posts of Foreign Secretary or Home Secretary, one of which he had believed was within his grasp during his coalition negotiations with Edward Heath.

It was in February 1982, nearly three years after the end of the trial, when the search for a meaningful role appeared to have reached a successful conclusion. It was widely reported that Jeremy Thorpe was to become director of the British section of Amnesty International, the London-based non-governmental organisation focused on human rights. The mission of the organisation is to campaign for 'a world in which every person enjoys all of the human rights enshrined in the Universal Declaration of Human Rights and other international human rights instruments' – sentiments which sat comfortably with the policies for which Jeremy Thorpe had campaigned forcefully during his political career.

In support of his application for the job he contended that he had already effectively carried out a mission for Amnesty – a trip he made to Ghana in the 1970s when he visited prisoners and lobbied the Ghanaian government over the plight of political prisoners in the former British possession.

When the appointment became widely known, it triggered a backlash among the Amnesty membership, with the most telling intervention coming from one of the founders of the organisation, David Astor, editor of the *Observer*, a Sunday newspaper sympathetic to the Liberal party. Astor's objection to the appointment must have been particularly galling to Jeremy Thorpe, coming as it did from a man with the same sort of deeply liberal views on social issues, and whose passionate espousal of progressive causes – the plight of black Africans, the violation of human rights, and opposition to the death penalty, mirrored Thorpe's own beliefs.

Astor was the third child of American-born English parents, Waldorf Astor and Nancy Witcher Langhorne. The product of an immensely wealthy business dynasty, and raised in the grandeur of a great country estate where the political and intellectual elite gathered, he nevertheless showed compassion for the poor and opposed what he saw as destructive socioeconomic policies.

In 1937 Astor joined the *Observer*, then owned by his father and went on to edit the paper for 27 years. On his death in 2001 the *Daily Telegraph's* obituary said that he had transformed the newspaper from 'a staid organ of the Establishment into the leading forum of English liberalism'. Although in many ways a diffident man, those close to Astor recognised that he had a core of steel, and he had no hesitation in putting the knife into Jeremy Thorpe over the Amnesty post. His contention that the former Liberal leader was effectively damaged goods proved fatal to Thorpe's chances of survival with Amnesty.

On 27 February 1982, Astor declared publicly that Thorpe was not the man for the Amnesty job. The post, he said, rested on its reputation for good judgement. Astor added: "Jeremy's reputation has gone through some troubles. He has not shown himself to be a man of good judgement."

At the end of February '82 the Amnesty ruling council in Britain voted 11-9 in favour of allowing Jeremy Thorpe to continue in the role of director. However, the council also proposed to ask its 18,000 members if they agreed with the decision. The council would consider the response at the end of March. Six days before he was to take up the post, on 5 March, Thorpe resigned from Amnesty. His leaving statement implied that the organisation itself had been through troubled times in the recent past and he seemed to suggest that the objections to his continuing as director came from a minority of members. The statement read: "I have no wish to perpetuate Amnesty's history of conflict over recent years. A minority of members have shown that they will continue to try and undermine my position."

The ever-loyal Peter Bray had no doubt that in resigning from the post Jeremy Thorpe had sacrificed his own interests for the wider good, telling the press: "He has put Amnesty International before himself, which is a great gesture from a man who was ideal for the job."

Thorpe did retain one influential post, his position as chairman of the political committee of the United Nations Association. But the progression of Parkinson's Disease led to his withdrawal by the mid-1980s from what little remained of his public activity.

Time can be a great healer and there is evidence that Thorpe himself believed that feelings towards him had gradually become more charitable as the years went by. In 1987 he was offered, and accepted, the honorary presidency of the North Devon Liberal Association, which became the Liberal Democrat Association, formed after the Liberal-SDP merger.

Throughout the years of allegations, the trial and the 1979 General Election defeat, the loyalty of so many of the party activists in North Devon had never been seriously in question. Nationally, although the attitude of the national leadership of the Liberals and subsequently the Liberal Democrats was to soften, the determination to exclude him from the political arena never slackened.

One route back to political activity would have been a life peerage in the House of Lords, and friends apparently lobbied the party leadership on his behalf, but in vain. It is believed that he then turned to the Labour Party in the hope of a nomination, but again met rejection, Tony Blair apparently considering it was no part of his role to gain honours for members of a rival political organisation.

Thorpe continued to have a hold over the membership of the party. With the trial now 20 years behind him and the Liberals, he attended the 1997 annual conference and received a standing ovation. Public opinion on most major social issues became ever more radical and in 2008 Jeremy told the *Guardian* newspaper. "If it (the Norman Scott affair) happened now I think ... the public would be kinder. Back then they were very troubled by it; it offended their set of values."

In 1996, Scott Freeman and Barrie Penrose had published *Rinkagate: Rise and Fall of Jeremy Thorpe*, an effort to merge previously published accounts into a single volume, which contained a detailed description of Thorpe's then current medical condition. The resulting media attention in Britain has been cited as a reason for Thorpe's son Rupert's decision to leave the country and work as a photographer in the United States. In 1999 Jeremy Thorpe himself published an anecdotal memoir, *In My Own Time*. He repeated his denial of any sexual relationship with Scott and maintained that the decision not to offer evidence was made to avoid prolonging the trial, since it was clear that the prosecution's case was "shot through with lies, inaccuracies and admissions".

In the 2005 General Election campaign Thorpe appeared on television, attacking both the Conservative and Labour parties for supporting the Iraq war. Three years later, in 2008, he gave interviews to the *Guardian* and to the *Journal of Liberal History*. York Membery, the Liberal journal's interviewer, found Thorpe able to communicate only in a barely audible whisper, but with his brain power unimpaired.

Thorpe asserted that he 'still had steam in my pipes'; reviewing the current political situation, he considered the Labour prime minister Gordon Brown 'dour and unimpressive', and dubbed the Conservative leader David Cameron "a phoney ... a Thatcherite trying to appear progressive".

Despite the passage of the years and the inexorable progression of Parkinson's disease, the barbed wit which made him a feared debater and political opponent remained undiminished.

PART TWO
Jeremy Thorpe and North Devon

As the Member of Parliament for the North Devon constituency and leader of the Liberal Party, Jeremy Thorpe was constantly in contact with five main groups of individuals, each with a different stake in the politician's life and work.

The first group, those who came closest to observing the MP on a regular basis, both at times of great and joyful success and again when fortune turned away, causing sadness and stress, were headed by the fellow Liberals who were professionally responsible for organising his election campaigns and his activities between polls, the periods known to Lilian Prowse, his full-time agent in North Devon and her assistant Peter Bray, as 'peacetime'.

A 'sub group' of professionals, who by virtue of their callings enjoyed a close access to the MP, were the journalists, employed by local, regional and national newspapers, radio and television stations, who covered his activities, and the photographers who shot some of the famous, often quirky photographs which helped to establish the Thorpe legend.

The second group, who again saw Jeremy Thorpe behind closed doors, were his fellow Liberal MPs and Peers, the party's officials and administrators at both national and regional level, and the mass of Liberal party activists, the constituency officials, branch officers, and elected councillors at city, district and county level. All of these people, like the professionals around him, would at times have had privileged access to Thorpe close-up, in situations of both triumph and tragedy, as opposed to the general public who saw only the wonderfully charismatic politician on the stump in the towns and villages of North Devon, the man who seemed to recognise every individual and was adept at convincing them that each brief conversation was a highlight of his day.

The same public comprised the third grouping, the voters, people who, in his capacity as leader turned out to see Jeremy on his whistle stop tours of the country, particularly in those areas with a strong Liberal tradition from Cornwall in the far south west to Orkney and Shetland, and from the shores of Cardigan Bay in Wales to the Isle of Ely in East Anglia – all areas which returned Liberal Members of Parliament during his years at the party helm.

His own electorate, the voters of North Devon, naturally saw him far more frequently than those elsewhere and many of them have vivid memories of their MP bounding up to them in the streets of Barnstaple, South Molton, Ilfracombe and elsewhere, greeting them like long lost friends and using his phenomenal memory (and taking advantage of detailed briefings from his staff before any walkabout) to display a detailed knowledge of their lives.

Whether Liberal voters or not, there were few people who came into conversation with Jeremy Thorpe who would not have been proud to tell their families and friends that he had shaken their hands that day when he dropped into villages like Chittlehampton, High Bickington or Filleigh.

The fourth group able to observe Jeremy Thorpe at reasonably close quarters, and in particular at the often tense post-polling counts, when all the campaign predictions counted for nothing against the hard facts of the votes actually cast, were his political opponents. Naturally, given the facts of life in politics in most rural seats, the main protagonists at North Devon election contests were the Liberals and the Conservatives, with the Labour Party the only other political organisation to oppose Thorpe at each of his North Devon contests, from his first election to the seat in 1959 to his defeat 20 years later.

Given the fact that Thorpe's last contest was almost 40 years ago, most of his opponents for a seat at Westminster have passed on, although at least one Labour candidate, in his early twenties at the time, still marvels at how the Liberal managed to attract such support from an electorate which in general disagreed with many of his beliefs and declared policies.

6. Thorpe and the Professionals

Jeremy Thorpe was exceptionally well served by the professionals who masterminded his election campaigns and supported his day-to-day work in both his constituency and at Westminster. And when it came to his dealings with the media, his flamboyance and articulacy made it odds on that any encounter would produce a worthwhile headline and an out-of-the ordinary picture.

Despite the lapse of time since the heyday of Thorpe's political career, there are still many people, in all categories and walks of life, who have first hand recollections of the man. In the instances of those who are no longer with us, many have left on record their impressions of a master politician at work.

Jeremy Thorpe was at all times the first to acknowledge that his electoral success depended to a great extent on the professional agents who worked with him on his home ground in North Devon. Both Lilian Prowse and Peter Bray served Thorpe and the Liberal party as full-time agents; both, in their own different ways, became legends within the Liberal party and the wider political world.

Lilian Prowse and her husband Jack were the mainstays of the North Devon Constituency Liberal Association for close on 30 years. As related in Chapter 2, *Thorpe's road to North Devon,* it was Jack Prowse who stiffened the backbones of the despairing constituency party following the local Liberals' worst-ever General Election performance in 1951. Jack agreed to take on more work and responsibility for re-building shattered party morale, and committed his wife to the cause with the almost throwaway line that she would, 'type a few letters and that sort of thing'.

Barnstaple-born, and from a traditional Liberal and Methodist background, Lilian attended Barnstaple Grammar School for Girls but, when she was barely in her teens, suffered the loss through illness of her mother and had the extra responsibility of helping her father to run the home. After leaving school she worked in the offices of a leading local car dealer, County Motors, which no doubt supplied the typing experience her husband had decided should be turned to the advantage of the Liberal party.

Jack, also Barnstaple born, was an insurance agent, working for the Prudential, and he had a minute knowledge of the constituency, gained from constantly travelling around the towns and villages. The administrative skills Lilian was to quickly demonstrate and Jack's contacts with the local voters were a formidable combination and were soon to produce a transformation in the party's fortunes across North Devon.

At the same time as Lilian's work for the Liberal Party began to increase – the voluntary work became a job as part-time agent in 1956 and a full-time post in 1958 – her homemaking skills were also being fully utilised. Jack and Lilian had four children, who share memories of growing up in a happy home but one distinguished from those of their friends by its deeply political atmosphere and the chance that, on their return from school, they might find a well-known politician enjoying a cup of tea in their mother's kitchen.

Of the four children, three have been politically active. Liz is a mainstay of the local Liberal Association to this day and is married to North Devon councillor Derrick Spear. Richard has also served as a councillor in the Liberal cause, whilst youngest child Malcolm led North Devon Council for a record length of time. Margaret left North Devon when it became time to go away to college, but still remembers the bustle of home life in a political family. Malcolm also built up a reputation as an election agent, using the techniques he had observed so closely in North Devon to improve the chances of Liberal successes elsewhere in the country.

Media profiles of Lilian Prowse often marvelled at how she combined such a rigorous post, with such an ambitious and dynamic character as Jeremy Thorpe, with being the mother of four children. Her response to the inevitable question was simple: "The job absolutely filled my life, although I managed to dovetail it in somehow with my private life.

"They were happy years. The election campaigns were exciting and fulfilling and I always had wonderful support in the constituency. The job enabled me to form many friendships."

Much of the Prowse energy in the early years was concentrated on building up a local party organisation unrivalled anywhere else, which eventually resulted in a network of more than 50 town and village branches. Three years after Lilian's appointment as part-time agent, and just a year after she was able to tackle the task on a full-time basis, came Jeremy Thorpe's first election success, when he won North Devon, albeit by the tiny majority of 362 votes.

One of the most important factors in achieving success of any kind is self-belief. With Jeremy Thorpe as candidate and Lilian Prowse as the power behind the throne, the material produced by the North Devon Association in the four years between Thorpe's first, unsuccessful, attempt to win the seat in 1955 and his eventual narrow win in 1959, simply oozes confidence at a stage at which many politicians might have been wary about putting up too many hostages to fortune.

The theme of the leaflet, entitled *Five Years Progress* is a celebration of Thorpe's five years as candidate. It is in many ways an astonishing document; the sort of publication one might expect a political party to publish *after* rather than before winning an election. It is effectively a declaration to the political and wider worlds in North Devon that the Liberal Party, considered to be a corpse after the 1951 General Election humiliation was actually alive, well and kicking very hard.

The booklet carries messages of support and encouragement from just about anyone who was anybody in the Liberals ranks of the time, from the party's national President, Leonard Behrens, Lord Rea, the leader of the Liberal Peers, the party leader, Jo Grimond, Lord Beveridge, the architect of the welfare state and former Liberal MP for Berwick-on-Tweed, and party worthies including Isaac Foot, Lady Violet Bonham Carter, the famed cricket writer and poet

John Arlott, then Liberal Prospective Candidate for Epping, and broadcaster Kenneth Wolstenhome, another supporter of the cause.

In his message Arlott shows remarkable prescience in forecasting victory for Thorpe at the next election, assuring the local party that theirs indeed was 'the key constituency.'

Jeremy Thorpe's success in 1959 not surprisingly ranked high in Lilian Prowse's memories of her years as agent. Her role assumed even greater importance when Jeremy was elected leader of the Liberal Party in 1967 and she took on the demanding task of co-ordinating his leadership activities with his constituency work, bringing her into close contact with Liberal headquarters in London and Thorpe's Westminster staff. Her developing expertise and growing reputation meant that she was closely involved with the party's scheme for training agents in the 1960s and her work was recognised in 1972 when she was awarded the MBE for services to politics.

Jeremy Thorpe's role as leader also led to a significant increase in demands for his time from the media. Derek Henderson of the *North Devon Journal*, one of the journalists closest to Thorpe and his team for many years, explained: "Lilian Prowse became a nationally-important contact for journalists in both Fleet Street and abroad as the direct link with Thorpe, who for ten of Lilian's 24 years in the job led his party.

"Several times during the high spots of her career her office in the Liberal headquarters in Cross Street, Barnstaple, became the focal point for the world's political press. But through it all she never forgot her basic duty – the sympathetic link between the North Devon electorate and their MP."

Lilian Prowse's public life, Henderson added, was 'inexorably bound up with that of Jeremy Thorpe and his colourful career', adding: "But she was a personality and character in her own right. Much of the credit for his election successes was put down to her efficient and painstaking organisational ability."

The local party's success in building up a network of branches, which became adept fundraisers in their own right, meant that the North Devon constituency at its peak employed not only a full-time agent but also an assistant agent and a secretary also working full-time. The assistant was Peter Bray, who benefitted from having a leading contributor to the Liberal's national training scheme for agents working on a daily basis at the next desk to his own.

Like Jack and Lilian Prowse, Peter Bray, still a well-known and frequently recognised figure in Barnstaple, is a North Devonian through and through. After leaving the then North Devon Technical College in 1959, the year of Jeremy Thorpe's first electoral triumph, he worked as a clerk for a local building firm until moving into the motor trade. His real vocation lay in the world of politics and he was a Liberal councillor on the former Barnstaple Borough Council and later on Barnstaple Town Council, serving as deputy mayor in 1976-77. He cut his teeth working for the return of Jeremy Thorpe at the General Election of 1970, and was appointed as assistant to Lilian Prowse the following year, a job he held until her retirement in 1980, when he succeeded her as agent, remaining in post for five years.

His sterling work in North Devon notwithstanding, Peter's greatest political fame stems from the reputation he built in the 1970s and 1980s as the Liberal Party's 'by-election supremo.' At the time the party was on the attack and Bray's very name was enough to strike fear into the hearts of both Conservative and Labour agents facing mid-term elections, often when their local party's fortunes were in decline.

In an echo of the Oxford University 'commandos' led by the undergraduate Jeremy Thorpe in the late '40s and '50s, Bray's raiders stiffened the Liberal ranks, often in constituencies where the party had only the most minimal organisation. National newspaper headlines across a swathe of the media from the Liberal-leaning *Guardian* to the Tory *Daily Mail* and the august *Times* proclaimed the activities of 'The Bray Gang' and the 'Liberal street fighters on dawn patrol.'

Bray's battle honours included his roles as either election agent or assistant agent/area organiser – 'on loan' from North Devon – at ten by-elections between 1976 and 1982, a fruitful time for the Liberals at mid-term contests. In addition he worked for Thorpe in North Devon at the General Elections of 1970, 1974 (February and October) and 1979, and for Thorpe's successor as candidate, Roger Blackmore in 1983. He was agent for Liberal candidate Michael Aza Pinney at the election for the European Parliament in 1979 and performed the same role for Peter Driver in 1984.

Peter Bray was part of a Liberal winning team at some of the most famous by-elections of the twentieth century. He worked to elect Liberal candidates at the Rochdale and Uxbridge mid-term contests in 1972 and Berwick-upon-Tweed in 1973 and at Beaconsfield in 1982. His experience helped former Labour minister and joint Social Democratic party founder Roy Jenkins to victory as the Liberal/SDP Alliance candidate at Glasgow Hillhead in '82 but his greatest triumph was yet to come.

In late 1982 Bray was drafted in as election agent for another Alliance candidate, Simon Hughes, in Bermondsey, in the heart of London's docklands. Hughes was a Liberal and as the campaign unfolded *The Times* described the campaigning as having 'all the hallmarks of Liberal rather than SDP techniques'. The seat looked virtually impregnable for Labour but turned out to be the Liberal triumph that really sealed Bray's reputation nationally.

Bermondsey had been held for Labour for almost four decades by Bob Mellish, an old-style Labour man from a working class background – his father was a docker. Bob worked for the Transport and General Workers Union after leaving school and during World War Two fought against the Japanese in South-East Asia. The votes of Transport Workers' delegates to what was then the Rotherhithe constituency won him the nomination and he easily won the seat, which was later re-named Bermondsey.

A tough Labour chief whip from 1969-70 and again from 1974 to 1976, , he held ministerial posts for Housing and Local Government in Harold Wilson's governments. Mellish, whose views on issues such as immigration and nuclear weapons were well to the right of the party, was concerned by the shift to the left within Labour nationally. When his own constituency party was taken over by left-wing hardliners, conflict became inevitable.

Rupert growing up. The Thorpes at Cobbaton.
(North Devon Liberal Association Archive)

Jeremy and Marion on the stump in Chittlehampton, a village with strong Liberal traditions. *(North Devon Liberal Association Archive)*

As the pressures increased Thorpe, seen here in reflective mood, relied more and more for release upon on his country retreat in North Devon. *(North Devon Liberal Association Archive)*

David Steel (left), who succeeded Thorpe as Liberal leader, pictured with his predecessor at the unveiling of a portrait of Jeremy at the National Liberal Club. Pictured next to Jeremy is Michael Aza Pinney, who contested North Devon for the Liberals in 1987. *(Rupert Thorpe)*

A celebratory pint for Jeremy Thorpe. *(North Devon Liberal Association Archive)*

Jeremy Thorpe, as always immaculately dressed, greets the crowds on landing from a hovercraft. Pictured left is John Pardoe MP, with a representative of the hovercraft firm in the centre. *(North Devon Liberal Association Archive)*

Above left: The Hovercraft tour. Pictured l-r are Derrick Spear, Lilian Prowse's son in law, Paul Tyler, John Pardoe and Jeremy. *(Derrick and Liz Spear)*

Above right: Jeremy, Marion and Rupert on the deck of the Hovercraft. *(Derrick and Liz Spear)*

Jeremy Thorpe on walkabout in North Devon.

A Christmas card sent by the Thorpe family, showing Jeremy, Marion and the young Rupert in an (unseasonal) beach setting. *(North Devon Liberal Association Archive)*

The memorial to Caroline Thorpe on Codden Hill, near Bishop's Tawton, in the North Devon constituency. *(Author)*

From 1971 onwards North Devon had a full-time assistant agent. Peter Bray worked with Lilian Prowse and took over from her as Constituency Agent when she retired, overseeing the eventual regaining of the seat by Nick Harvey. Bray, seen here with the scrapbooks covering his long and successful carerer, masterminded several famous Liberal and Liberal/SDP Alliance by-election victories across Britain. *(Tony Gussin/*North Devon Gazette*)*

One of the last photographs of Jeremy Thorpe to be taken in his constituency. He and Marion visited The Caroline Thorpe Ward at North Devon Hospital to present equipment. *(North Devon Gazette)*

From: The Rt. Hon. Jeremy Thorpe, M.P.

Dec 18. 1974.

HOUSE OF COMMONS
LONDON SWIA OAA

Dearest Lilian

with so

many many thanks

affectionately

Jeremy

You will look like

an arch-duchess!

A final letter of appreciation written by Jeremy Thorpe to his agent Lilian Prowse.

When he decided not to stand for Parliament again, the local party rejected his preferred successor and selected its secretary, the left-wing Peter Tatchell. Although Labour and its current leader Michael Foot initially declined to endorse Tatchell's candidature, he was eventually adopted. Mellish quit the party in 1982 and for a while sat in the House of Commons as an Independent but resigned his seat later in the year, paving the way for a by-election.

This took place on 24 February 1983 and the result still resonates today. *The Times* reported from Bermondsey on the morning before polling day, describing how 'a dawn patrol of young Liberal activists' visited every home in the compact urban constituency, 'in a final attempt to fulfil the bookmakers' forecast of a shock victory for their candidate.'

Leaflets being pushed through every door urging support for Liberal candidate Simon Hughes were, said *The Times*, the last detail of a plan worked out by Liberal strategists before Christmas. For weeks the Alliance campaign had been masterminded by Peter Bray from the third floor above an empty hardware shop in a typically run-down south east London street. Bray's task had been to co-ordinate the efforts of a dozen full-time volunteers, swelled at weekends by up to 900 helpers.

Bray told the newspaper: "My main enjoyment is organisation as opposed to aspiring to become an MP. I aspire to get MPs and councillors elected, and that is my vocation in life. I always try to make a campaign as happy as possible. People laugh at me when I say that but I think there is nothing better than a team whose members get on well together and enjoy what they are doing."

On the wall of Bray's campaign headquarters was a copy of a joke leaflet produced by his Liberal colleagues. The leaflet was headed "Wanted: The Bray Gang. Feared throughout the Wild West (Devon and Cornwall), for their legendary raids on inns, hostelries, breweries and Liberal clubs."

When the votes were counted in Bermondsey Bob Mellish's former Labour majority of 11,000 had been turned into a Liberal majority of 11,000. The swing of 44.2 per cent to the Liberals remains the largest by-election swing in history and ensured Peter Bray's place in the history of British politics. Bray was understandably cock-a-hoop at the result but had to work hard to play down claims that the Liberals had fought a vicious smear campaign or that Tatchell's rout was achieved through press hysteria, largely fuelled by his activities with the Gay Liberation Front – something which, like the justifiable fears that an accusation of homosexuality would end Jeremy Thorpe's political career, would today hardly raise an eyebrow.

Understandably, there were high hopes that the success achieved in Bermondsey by Simon Hughes could be repeated at the General Election later in 1983 by Roger Blackmore, the successor to Jeremy Thorpe as Liberal candidate in North Devon. It was not to be. The Conservative Tony Speller retained the seat in with a very slightly increased majority compared to his 1979 success. Speller was again successful in 1987, albeit with a considerably reduced majority and the Liberals had to wait until 1992 for victory, achieved by Nick Harvey.

In the early 1980s the North Devon glory years of Jeremy Thorpe, Lilian Prowse and Peter Bray were over for the time being. In 1984 the media reported that rising costs had forced the North Devon Association to dispense with the services of a full-time agent. The candidate, Roger Blackmore, had already said goodbye to the constituency after his June 1983 defeat and the next man in line to try and restore Liberal glories, David Short, a city councillor in Hereford, did not in the event stay long enough to contest an election.

Looking back recently on his 14 years as Liberal agent in North Devon, with the BBC dramatisation of the Norman Scott affair a topic on many lips, Peter recalled Jeremy Thorpe as 'a great man who was a leader on the national stage but also a deeply caring local MP and a huge force for good in North Devon'.

He said: "I remember Jeremy as he was – he was a much-respected MP and the sort of bloke you could walk through Barnstaple with and everybody knew him, talked to him and he knew a lot of peoples' names. He was a friend and he treated you like any other person, he was never superior and I had a lot of laughs with him. He left behind a lasting legacy and was responsible for some of North Devon's modern landmarks – he campaigned for North Devon District Hospital, which opened in 1979 and for the North Devon Link Road.

Peter, who admitted that the television programme proved 'hurtful' for many people who had known Thorpe, added: "North Devon has not changed a tremendous amount over the years but it's a lot better than it was when Jeremy was first elected, and I am sure it gained a lot from him being the MP."

Throughout his active political career, and periodically after his retirement from public life, Jeremy Thorpe was news and many journalists and broadcaster who later found fame in their chosen trade cut their teeth in North Devon. Among those who found their way to Cross Street were Max Hastings, son of the early television personality Macdonald Hastings. Max, later editor of the *Daily Telegraph,* who became a household name when reporting the Falklands War joined Thorpe on the campaign trail leading up to the 1979 General Election, when the looming shadow of the Old Bailey trial was attracting more journalists than ever to North Devon

In 1974, in a happier era for North Devon Liberals another leading journalist had ventured into the constituency to cover the run-up to a General Election for *The Times*. Caroline Moorehead OBE has enjoyed a distinguished career as biographer, historian, human rights journalist and literary critic. She is a trustee and director of Index on Censorship and a governor of the British Institute of Human Rights, and also helped to start a legal advice centre for asylum seekers from the Horn of Africa in Cairo. All these pursuits would undoubtedly have won the approval of Jeremy Thorpe.

In February 1974, as the United Kingdom faced what was to prove to be the first of two extremely close General Elections in the space of the calendar year, Moorehead, as a 30-year-old aspiring journalist and writer was sent to follow the party workers campaigning in the three Parliamentary constituencies held by the leaders of the main political parties.

Observing the proprieties her articles, trailed by the headline writers as taking a lighter view of the election ballyhoo, started off with the agent of the current occupier of 10 Downing Street, Conservative Edward Heath, followed on with a visit to the Huyton, Liverpool constituency of Harold Wilson, and finally ended up in Barnstaple, with a relatively small focus on North Devon and Jeremy Thorpe. Although the portion of Caroline Moorehead's article devoted to Thorpe and North Devon may have been small, in proportion to the Liberal Party's Parliamentary representation, her perception of how the constituency worked was acute. It was made plain that Jeremy Thorpe dominated to an unusual degree and that his appeal was very largely a personal affair.

Moorehead commented at the start of the North Devon section of the article that although Messrs Wilson and Heath were regarded by their party supporters as good constituency members, and were punctilious about holding surgeries for constituents, her talks with the Sidcup and Huyton agents and voluntary workers had produced few actual mentions of the Prime Minister and the Leader of the Opposition.

One person she had interviewed had said that both Heath and Wilson simply ran the show 'like ghost candidates'. The situation was very different in Barnstaple where, she discovered: "All anyone ever talks about is Jeremy."

One party worker quoted in *The Times* article proclaimed. "Jeremy is the Liberal Party. We want your support for Jeremy, is what the canvassers say on the doorsteps."

Caroline Moorehead reported how the personalised campaign theme was evident on her arrival at the Liberal HQ in Barnstaple, where a huge yellow banner strung above the door to the Liberal Club and offices proclaimed 'Thorpe is the man! Inside the offices Lilian Prowse agreed with the general assessment that the campaign was a very personal one. "They feel around here that Jeremy belongs to them," she told the journalist.

Mrs Prowse, *The Times* reported, had plenty of help in running the campaign. Assistant Peter Bray was present, 'loyally dressed' in a yellow shirt and purple tie; and there was also a full-time secretary and two part-time helpers, Jeremy Thorpe's two secretaries had temporarily moved their base from Westminster to Barnstaple, and a researcher and several additional people for office work completed the professional campaign strength.

Moorehead concluded that such a team was necessary, if unusually lavish for a Liberal MP, party leader or not, saying: "The constituency is enormous, nearly 600 square miles, with 60 local branches and 73,000 electors on the register." Because of the size of the area, canvassing was being handled locally, with the roving help of the '400-500 Young Liberal members in the constituency'.

The national media usually only made it to Barnstaple for General Elections or when there was a hint (or more) of scandal in the air. The local press were there all the time. Jeremy Thorpe, Lilian Prowse and Peter Bray, always alive to the primary need to keep the North Devon public onside, made sure that the big names from London were never allowed to elbow their provincial counterparts to one side.

One press man ever-present during Thorpe's two decades as an MP was local man Tony Freeman, who at 78 and living in Shirwell, North Devon, keeps his photography and public relations skills up-to-date in an age when technology has transformed the media scene.

The Barnstaple media in the 1950s and 1960s operated out of offices in the High Street, with premises that ran all the way back to the River Taw waterfront at The Strand, where the large reels of newsprint were offloaded and stored for the on-site printing works. The offices represented a media empire in miniature, with not just the *North Devon Journal Herald* editorial team but also reporters and photographers representing the *Express and Echo*, the Exeter-based evening paper and the influential *Western Morning News (WMN)*, all owned by the same company.

In the days before the proliferation of broadcast media, the internet and news and sports results delivered almost instantly to smart phones and other devices, the public relied to an extent almost unimaginable today upon newspapers. The *Western Morning News* early in the day and the *Express and Echo*, published in the afternoon, were delivered to Barnstaple (as the *WMN* is to this day). The afternoon paper was sold on the streets and the High Street offices contained a machine to print the latest news and racing results into a space left blank when the paper was originally printed in Exeter – the Stop Press column.

Tony Freeman got his first job in the Barnstaple office of the *Express and Echo* after leaving school in Barnstaple in the late 1950s. He was just in time to help cover the victory of Jeremy Thorpe at the 1959 General Election, helping to capture in print and on film the euphoria of the local Liberals and the excitement and spectacle of the torchlight procession through the town.

For the next 10 years he photographed Thorpe on many, many occasions, explaining: "The Barnstaple MP and later Liberal Party leader was a photographer's dream, jumping over hurdles, helping out at lamb roasts, addressing packed crowds at events in the Barnstaple Pannier Market and elsewhere. Being Jeremy, he was always flamboyantly dressed, with that famous brown trilby hat. The media love an image that is different, and Thorpe always delivered. Jeremy was acutely aware of the need to cultivate his local roots and he always gave the Devon-based media preferential treatment."

As Thorpe's national and international profile expanded, there was a growing demand for pictures. Freeman established a freelance business with another local man, Paul Harris, handling both news and commercial photography. "We established a studio in Joy Street for the company, Waverley Photographic. For our launch Jeremy and the nanny brought the three-month-old Rupert along and Roger and I photographed him lying virtually naked on a blanket, as you did at the time with babies, whilst his father opened the Liberal Fête in the Pannier Market. More than 20 years later I asked Rupert whether he would give us a repeat performance but he wasn't too keen!

"When Jeremy returned we took some superb pictures of him hoisting Rupert up in the air in a typically boisterous fashion. That inaugurated our new business venture and we sold the picture to all the national newspapers, including the Communist party paper, the *Daily Worker*, which didn't usually go in for that sort of thing."

There is ample evidence that Jeremy Thorpe appreciated the importance of a good relationship with the media more than most. But whilst many politicians and others in the public eye maintain that relationship when the going is good, when times get harder they often tend to close the door and withdraw co-operation. Not Jeremy Thorpe.

During the months prior to the Old Bailey trial in 1979, during the committal proceedings at Minehead and all through the trauma of having to fight a General Election campaign with the threat of prison hanging over his head, Thorpe maintained a cool and professional approach towards the reporters, photographers and TV crews who followed him wherever he went.

Tony Freeman was one of the jostling press pack, and as a freelance taking images for newspapers, magazines and Independent Television News at every possible opportunity, with tight deadlines and impatient, demanding news and picture editors to satisfy, he had to be ruthless in his pursuit of the man he had previously photographed on far happier occasions.

He recalls: "To be honest I was 'monstering' Jeremy, as the word goes in the business. In the lead-up to the trial, when the allegations were public knowledge, Jeremy built a high fence at his home at Chuggaton, to try and get some privacy. I got hold of a horsebox and stood on top to get pictures."

On one occasion during the Minehead court hearings Freeman was involved in a car accident. Despite suffering some concussion, he pressed on to the court, getting a lift from another journalist. With job done, he returned home in the evening. "There was a knock on the door and who should be standing there but Jeremy Thorpe, come to check that I was OK.

"Unbelievable. When you imagine what the man was going through and the fact that I was one of the media people dogging his every footstep, he could have been excused for being nothing more than coldly polite, at the very most. Yet here he was, despite his own problems, concerned about how I was feeling. He appeared to take it all in his stride. Absolutely incredible."

After the trial verdict, Thorpe invited just two photographers to his Higher Chuggaton cottage to take photographs of himself, Marion and Rupert. Tony Freeman and Tom Moon, the Barnstaple-based photographer for the *Western Morning News*, were the privileged pair.

Tony Freeman has heard all the conspiracy theories that have been aired over the years in respect of the Thorpe affair. He keeps his own counsel on most of them but admits to having thought deeply about the claims that the South African authorities during the apartheid era were involved in stirring up trouble for the Liberal leader.

"Jeremy was well known for his anti-colonial policies and in addition to that, he supported strong sanctions against Rhodesia, when the Ian Smith regime declared unilateral independence, even suggesting that Britain should carry out bombing raids. What I do know is that on at least two occasions myself and other media people received anonymous 'deep throat' style telephone calls alerting us to the fact that sensational revelations were to be made on that or the next day in court hearings.

"We will never know where those tip-offs came from. Of course, we always acted on them, and we were not disappointed."

Tony Freeman had more opportunities than most over the years to observe Jeremy Thorpe when he was on public view, under all conditions. His verdict today could not be plainer. "He was a very clever man, and he was well served by his professional colleagues. I travelled with him by helicopter in one of his national tours as party leader and saw him at work. He was briefed during the journeys on what he was about to see when we landed and on the people he would meet. It was impressive that, after just a hurried briefing he always performed so confidently. But during the difficult times, how he managed to keep going as he did is still difficult to understand."

During Thorpe's later years, he kept in touch with Freeman. "He always phoned me at Christmas, although in the latter years it became increasingly difficult for him to communicate because of his Parkinson's disease."

Freeman is one of the many people who remain impressed by Thorpe's achievements as an MP for North Devon. One of the most important to his mind is the action taken by the MP when the Church of Scientology showed an interest in acquiring Lundy Island. Freeman travelled to Lundy with representatives of the Church and believes that had it not been for prompt action by Thorpe the island would be in the organisation's ownership today.

"Jeremy persuaded the very wealthy Jack Hayward, who was a patriot and philanthropist and a Liberal sympathiser, of the importance of saving Lundy for the British people. Hayward subsequently gave £150,000 to allow the Landmark Trust to acquire Lundy and he later visited the island with Thorpe for a service of thanksgiving.

"All in all, Jeremy Thorpe was an incredible man," is Tony Freeman's verdict.

7. Through the Eyes of the Activists

Peter Bray is convinced that the Liberal Party's trademark technique of 'community politics' was conceived and nurtured in the market towns and villages of Jeremy Thorpe's North Devon constituency.

At the same time he readily admits that the actual name had probably not even been coined when he and Lilian Prowse were building up the local party branches – some 60 at the network's peak – which provided both the volunteer workers at election times and the funding for professionally-run campaigns.

The branches helped knit together the far-flung constituency and harnessed the skills and enthusiasm of voters sympathetic to the Liberal cause, who were made aware that they had a far greater role in the electoral process than simply turning up at a polling station and entering a cross on the ballot paper. Branch officials and members also acted as an efficient sounding board for recording the way the ordinary men and women in the street were thinking.

It was soon realised by a large section of the North Devon electorate that the Liberal Party locally was prepared to take the concept of active participation to new levels. In return for their help in raising funds and electing the MP, local voters were assured of a commitment to North Devon that ran far deeper than attendance at the occasional surgery and the odd visit to social events that represented the sum total of what some MPs in the major parties regarded as pulling their weight.

With reliable and imaginative backing from the political professionals developing such an effective network of activists across the community, Jeremy Thorpe could afford to divide his time between nursing (in the early days) and then representing the constituency, with pursuing his ambition to become a politician on the national and international stage.

He quite quickly built a national and international reputation for his knowledge of and passion for solving the issues of post-colonialism and apartheid. Yet despite being passionately concerned for the plight of the developing world, and in demand for his expertise in that field, virtually nothing was allowed to get in the way of his presence at what he and his helpers recognised were the key events of the constituency year.

The Liberal and Conservative fêtes held in Barnstaple Pannier Market were important landmark events in the North Devon year. On one occasion Thorpe, by now leader of the party, flew back especially from Persia (Iran) where he had been an official guest at the celebrations for the 2,500th anniversary of the Persian Monarchy, as represented by the final Shah (or King), the pro-Western and modernising Mohammad Reza Pahlavi, who reigned from September 1941 until he was deposed following a revolution in 1979, following clashes with Islamists and the country's communist party.

Drives through the night or in the early hours of the morning became part of the lives of Thorpe's agents. When the autumn party conference season coincided with the official opening of Barnstaple Fair, it meant a 350-mile dash from the Liberal Party Assembly at Scarborough to be one of the speakers at the ancient event. After a two-hour stay he was back on the road to North Yorkshire to rejoin the North Devon delegation of Lilian Prowse, Peter Bray and constituency party chairman Jim Isaac, a farmer from Chittlehampton.

Some party leaders might have avoided such a breakneck dash by hiding behind the cover of urgent business of state. Thorpe knew his constituents and knew the importance of an event of such ancient tradition.

Being a Liberal party activist in North Devon during the Thorpe era often meant much more than simply attending committee meetings, running a hoopla stall at a fete, or canvassing at elections. The techniques pioneered by the Prowse-Bray partnership put a remarkable amount of responsibility on to the branch association leaders. Most responded effectively, with some going far beyond what might normally be expected of volunteer workers.

Typical of the commitment (and ingenuity) of the volunteer workers was sales representative Albert Reed, secretary of the Sticklepath (Barnstaple) branch of the constituency party. Reed not only built up a remarkable membership total of 425 people in the 1970s but also developed a new way of bringing the party to the notice of newcomers to his patch. Between elections he carefully watched the local estate agents' lists. When a new family moved into the area he hurried around to their home to welcome them to the district and after obtaining their names, he sent the information to Thorpe's office. Within a few days the family would receive a letter, reading, 'Dear So and So, Welcome to my constituency'!

Political youth organisations had a much higher profile in the second half of the 20th century than appears to be the case today. The Young Conservatives – the definition of 'Young' in the late 1960s was 35 – had a reputation as being a first rate marriage bureau whilst the Young Socialists were somewhat more interested in the policies of their party.

In that same era the Young Liberal organisation nationally – at the time known officially as the National League of Young Liberals and founded in 1903 – hit the media headlines by adopting policies more usually associated with the political hard left. Active in Young Liberal politics on the national stage at this time was Peter Hain, later to join the Labour party, represent the South Wales constituency of Neath in the House of Commons from 1991 to 2015, and hold ministerial office in Tony Blair's governments.

Hain was the son of anti-apartheid activists of Scots descent in South Africa, where he grew up and was educated before coming to England to study at Queen Mary College, University of London, and the University of Sussex. Having joined the British anti-apartheid movement in 1967, a year later he joined the Liberal party and was both chairman and President of the Young Liberals. He gained worldwide fame as the chairman of the Stop the Seventies Tour campaign which disrupted tours by the South African rugby union and cricket teams in 1969 and 1970.

The stances of the Young Liberals of the era on international issues such as apartheid, Israel and the Vietnam War led to clashes with the national party, led by Jeremy Thorpe, who established a three-man commission which produced the Terrell Report, which accused some of the Young Liberals of being communists. The press at the time attached the description Red Guards to some of the more extreme youth wing members. Peter Hain was quoted as saying that many Young Liberals described themselves as 'libertarian socialists'.

Thorpe and the party became increasingly concerned that this stance was harming the Liberal image. The Young Liberals nationally were seen as becoming an electoral liability. In North Devon, and in the West Country as a whole, things were, predictably, rather different. Under a moderate leadership, the Young Liberals had been welded into a highly efficient campaigning machine. Key to the success of the organisation in the constituency and the region was a young schoolteacher with an impeccable Liberal pedigree and a track record of enlisting young people to the cause.

David Worden, born in 1948, grew up in Callington, Cornwall. His family were farmers, Methodists and staunch Liberal activists. David's earliest political memory is of milking a neighbouring farmer's cows whilst his own father helped voters get to their polling station during the 1955 General Election. He believes the Liberalism of his family was a logical step from their nonconformism, saying: "Liberalism and Methodism went hand in hand. All the members of the church I attended were good Liberals.

"There have been times when the Liberal party could simply have disappeared, but there has always been people who do not want to conform, who want to think for themselves. They have always seen the Liberal party as offering alternatives to the two other main political parties, who have over the years been in power, one or the other, for such a long time. That is the link between Liberalism and nonconformism".

David's next step on the road to political activism came at school, as he explains. "I was at Callington Grammar and in the run-up to the 1964 General Election the school staged a mock election. I was asked to stand as the Liberal candidate, and topped the poll. That wetted my appetite for politics".

He moved on to Westminster College, Oxford, which at the time was a teacher training college and college of higher education. The college was founded in London in 1851 as a training institute for teachers for Wesleyan Methodist schools, but moved to Oxford in 1959 and during David Worden's time its qualifications were awarded by Oxford University. In 2000, financial pressures caused the college to close. The Methodist Church subsequently leased the college's site at Harcourt Hill to Oxford Brookes University and it became the home of that university's Westminster Institute of Education.

David became involved with the Liberal Society, which boasted the largest membership of any society within the college. "We organised meetings with leading politicians, including David Steel. The meetings were broadly-based and on occasions we would invite not just Liberal speakers but people from the Conservatives and Labour parties too."

The speakers at Westminster College did not include Jeremy Thorpe but for David Worden a meeting with the Liberal Leader and North Devon MP was not long delayed. Thorpe's charisma and photographic memory was on display immediately, as David explains: "I met Jeremy for the first time quite soon after moving to North Devon in 1969, to take up my first teaching job. There was then a gap of six months before I came across him again. He knew me, knew what I was doing, and in fact knew practically everything there was to know about me! It was not a planned meeting and there was no-one at his shoulder to brief him. He just had an incredible memory and an obvious deep interest in the people he met."

David Worden's own political career began when he became a Liberal member of the former Barnstaple Borough Council in 1972, representing the old Trinity Ward. He retained his seat after the creation of the new North Devon District Council in 1974 and was a councillor until the 1980s, when a serious illness caused a gap in his political career. He moved to live in South Molton and stood successfully for election to the district council in the market town in 2007 and has been a member ever since. He is also a member of the South Molton Town Council.

His council membership ran in parallel to him accepting office in the Young Liberal organisation, and he was chairman not only of the Barnstaple branch but also of the party's youth wing in the whole of Devon and Cornwall. This led to an inevitable clash with the national organisation's increasingly extreme policies.

The methods used by the *Stop the Tour* activists did not go down well in rugby and cricket loving North Devon. David Worden says: "Jeremy Thorpe and the Young Liberals in North Devon were just as opposed to apartheid as their counterparts elsewhere. But tactics such as throwing tin tacks onto rugby pitches were certainly not approved."

David recalls a conference at Plymouth where the much more moderate West Country element of the Young Liberals hoped to change the leadership of the national body, with Worden himself slated to run for one of the vice-president posts up for election.

"People in North Devon and across the country felt that the actions of the national leadership were having a disastrous effect on the image of the Liberal Party. Our allies included David Alton, later the Liberal MP for Liverpool Edge Hill and Liverpool Mossley Hill, who was fiercely anti-apartheid but equally vehemently opposed to the methods being used by the more radical campaigners, widely believed to be bringing the party as a whole into disrepute. Others at the time trying to exert a calming influence included John Pardoe, MP for Truro from 1966 t0 1979 and a one-time deputy leader and later President of the Liberal Party, and David Penhaligon, Liberal MP for Truro from 1974 to 1986 who was seen as a potential future party leader until his death in a car accident.

"Unfortunately the over-enthusiasm of some of our West Country members sabotaged our efforts to achieve change. Many people signed up to call for change but it was discovered that numbers of those were not real young people. Apparently some people from North Cornwall had signed up their dogs! An inquiry was held and as a result I withdrew my nomination for a vice-presidency. I didn't want to get involved in scandal."

As a Methodist lay preacher, David Worden is well qualified to comment on the issue of whether or not the major reason for Jeremy Thorpe's defeat in the 1979 General Election, whilst awaiting trial on charges of conspiracy and incitement to murder, was his desertion by nonconformist voters. He says: "I did not see much evidence of this when I was out canvassing in 1979. But what I did find was a an unwillingness to commit themselves on the part of a lot of voters, a lot of sitting on the fence which had not been obvious in the past. People were saying things such as, 'well, I voted Liberal in the past', but they were saying it without giving much away about what they were going to do on this occasion."

"Probably many people who were upset by the revelations and the forthcoming trial decided to abstain, or they may have felt that, knowing I was a Methodist lay preacher myself, it was too sensitive an issue to discuss."

What does David Worden think are the reasons why Jeremy Thorpe has retained so much loyalty and affection in twenty-first-century North Devon. "Charisma is a word that is used on so many occasions but unless you actually experienced Jeremy in North Devon at the height of his powers it is understandable that people find it difficult to thoroughly understand what it meant.

"But apart from the charisma he really did great things for the constituency. Even his political opponents agreed that he was a very good constituency MP. The hospital, the link road and above all, the assisted area status that he fought for and won are the prime examples. As an MP he represented the whole electorate of North Devon not just the Liberal supporters, and people appreciated that fact."

8. In the View of the Voters

On the surface North Devon in 1959 was a very different place than it is today, as the end of the third decade of the twenty-first century approaches. But was it, deep down, really so very different? Or have the economic base of the area, the make-up of its population, the problems the constituency faces and the hopes of its people for the future remained remarkably constant over the passage of almost six decades?

It would be foolish to deny that there have been obvious changes to the day-to-day lives of North Devonians. Nearly 60 years after Jeremy Thorpe was first elected to represent the division in Parliament, it is difficult for a younger generation to imagine a society without mass car ownership, smart phones, and without vast national supermarket chains and out of town retail parks. Not to mention a society without drug and behavioural issues.

When Thorpe fought the 1959 General Election mobile phones and other electronic gadgets were the stuff of science fiction. Those households fortunate enough to possess a telephone, at a time when would-be consumers had to enter their names on a waiting list rather than simply go out and hand over the cash, had little difficulty in remembering their number, when the exchange was local and the numbers consisted of two or three digits. Advertisements of the period tell the story; Bideford 20, South Molton 59, Chittlehamholt 134 and Swimbridge 221 are actual examples of business phone numbers in use at the time.

In the market towns of the constituency, which in 1959 consisted of the boroughs of Barnstaple and South Molton, and their respective rural districts, together with the urban districts of Ilfracombe and Lynton, going shopping meant working your way through the main streets and connecting thoroughfares and, on market days, buying produce from the stalls in the pannier markets, from the wives of farmers and market gardeners who still sat in the market with their tables loaded with local produce.

Today's shoppers often regard making their way to the local supermarket and then packing their purchases into the boot of the family car as an unpleasant chore. In 1959 most shoppers from the rural villages and hamlets travelled into the towns by bus or even by train, before Dr Beeching recommended wholesale closure of rural railway branch lines or secondary routes. They carried their full shopping baskets from store to store, manhandled them to the bus stop or railway station, and even then often faced a longish haul to their homes where, no doubt, they enjoyed a well-earned cup of tea before packing their purchases away in store cupboards and cool larders – refrigerators, not to mention freezers, were still comparatively rare.

Whilst the women were usually left to do the shopping on their own – another huge societal change over the last half century and more – their men folk would congregate at the livestock markets (now sadly a thing of the past in Barnstaple), with much business also transacted in the nearby public houses. Goods services to the country railway stations were still in existence in the late 1950s, with foodstuffs for livestock, farm implements and general goods being delivered, and cattle sent away to Midland markets, notably at Banbury.

Overseas package holidays were in their infancy and most ordinary people had never flown in an aeroplane. Even in the best hotels guests shared bathrooms and in many bed and breakfast establishments a wash basin or even a bowl and a jug of water was the best the visitors could expect. Tourism was perhaps at its peak in the period in question, with long Saturdays-only trains of holidaymakers from the Midlands, the North and Southern England winding their way across Exmoor on the Taunton to Barnstaple route and via Exeter to Braunton and the steep haul up to Mortehoe and Woolacombe before an equally steep descent to Ilfracombe. Holidaymakers also found their way to Instow and Bideford, on the line to Torrington, with connecting bus services taking them to the seaside resorts and inland towns not directly served by rail.

The minority who had already joined the motor car revolution looked forward to their holidays but hardly relished the drive from their home areas to North Devon. The old A361 road from Taunton via Wiveliscombe, Bampton and South Molton was heavily-used and tortuous, with caravans towed by what would today be considered ridiculously under-powered saloon cars much in evidence. On summer Saturdays at the height of the season it was almost impossible for pedestrians to cross from one pavement to the other in roadside villages such as Swimbridge and Landkey.

And yet, despite all that has been lost and the major changes that have occurred in day-to-day life, an examination of the issues facing North Devon makes remarkably familiar reading even today. Voters enlisted by the North Devon Liberal Association in a long-running campaign to use the voices of ordinary people to illustrate the national and local issues of the day spoke of the things that still exercise the local electorate today; the rising cost of living, health provision, the difficulties of making farming pay, troubles with the unions, broken promises in the field of education, and the high taxes and business rates faced by the hotel, catering and other holiday industry sectors, all have a contemporary feel.

The influx of incomers, often but not always retired and particularly from the south-east of England, who would sell their properties for large sums of money and then inflate the prices in the local housing market, was an issue and Jeremy Thorpe and local politicians had to deal with the controversy of plans to relocate thousands of people from Greater London to North Devon.

The political world in 1959 was also, at least superficially, very different to the world of Theresa May, Jeremy Corbyn, Vince Cable and their 2018 followers although, again, many of the national issues which exercised the politicians and the general public half a century ago have not gone away, particularly in the contentious areas of Europe, the National Health Service and education.

Politics in the late 1950s and early '60s, during Jeremy Thorpe's first spell in the House of Commons, were still to some extent little different from the parliamentary landscape of the immediate post-World War Two era. Those born during the Edwardian era were still well represented in the House of Commons, whilst the House of Lords still had numerous representatives who had first seen the light of day under Queen Victoria.

During the spring and early summer of 1959, although Parliament was due to go into recess, the political parties were gearing up for a General Election, eventually called by Prime Minister Harold Macmillan for 8 October that year. It was in July 1959, speaking at Bedford, that Macmillan used the phrase that summed up an era of mounting material prosperity when he claimed that 'most of our people have never had it so good'. The Conservatives were duly victorious at the election, for a third time in a row, increasing their overall majority to 101. Margaret Thatcher was one of the new intake of Tory MPs, although for North Devonians the result that counted was Jeremy Thorpe's narrow victory (362 votes) over the sitting Conservative, James Lindsay – the Liberal party's only gain of the contest.

During that spring and summer of '59, the North Devon Liberal Association, with Thorpe as candidate, revived their fortunes and swept away the memory of being forced down to third place in 1951, worked ceaselessly for what they sensed was a possible victory, based on the charisma of Thorpe and the assiduous way he and his helpers had nursed the constituency since his first unsuccessful attempt to become its MP in '55.

With the prospect of a General Election becoming more and more likely, local Liberals set out to woo the electorate with a well planned and executed media campaign, tackling the issues of the day through the eyes of ordinary voters. The campaign was designed to keep the party faithful loyal and at the same time attract swing voters who saw a mirror image of themselves in the thoughts of the figures featured in the local newspapers.

Although the people featured in the media campaign were clearly committed Liberal voters and, in some cases at least, party activists, the advertorials were well enough constructed, avoiding too much overt propaganda, to be effective. Those selected to feature in the campaign were carefully chosen to reflect the big issues of the day, and covered a wide spectrum of North Devon society from local gentry, business people, through school teachers, hoteliers, bank employees, housewives and mothers, to farm labourers and trades unionists. The Young Liberal voice too, was included

A familiar weekend sight in Ilfracombe during the summer season of the late 1950s and early 1960s was the arrival of the holiday trains at the town's cliff top station, with a flood of new arrivals, heavily laden with luggage, flocking down the hill to seek bed and breakfast accommodation from the many establishments lining the route into the town. But even at this time, all was not well with the local tourist industry, a fact the North Devon Liberal strategists set out to exploit.

Harold Richardson, a local hotelier and a past President of Ilfracombe Chamber of Commerce accused the Conservative Government of doing 'little or nothing' to help North Devon's holiday resorts. Business rates and taxes remained unbearably high. Mr Richardson added: "As a hotelier I know the prosperity of our resort towns depends upon the holiday trade. If we are to continue to hold our own we must improve road and rail services and try and get more Government aid towards the capital development of the area – our local population is too small to do it alone. Our prime need is for an MP who will continually fight for these things in Parliament."

Lorry driver Arch Bodley of South Molton was a 'refugee' from the Labour party over the issue of what he deemed to be its extremist policies. He said: "The Labour party is OUT. Out of touch, out of date, out of favour and certainly out of North Devon politics. Their chief plank – nationalisation – is riddled with very dry rot and their stupidity in wanting to manufacture more H-bombs, with all its dangers, is another sign of their pink Toryism. Liberals want to see everyone owning something rather than the state owning everything. An active Liberal MP for North Devon would start the ball rolling."

Farmer Ken Sexon from Filleigh came out strongly in favour of the Devon and Cornwall Liberal Agricultural Report, saying: "This report would help farmers plan for future prosperity. Past governments have given only temporary relief against ever-present difficulties. The report wants farmers' costs to be reduced by blowing price rings and monopolies sky-high and also advocates channelling subsidies to the deserving. This would ensure the survival of the family farm, which has real value for our agricultural system. I hope all farmers will buy this report, for the prosperity of North Devon rests on the prosperity of the farm."

Farm worker Albert Sampson of Mariansleigh agreed with the view of the farmer. "We farm workers have never gone on strike to improve our conditions but there is a lot to be done if we are to stop the drift to the towns. Liberals want farm workers to get wages as good as those in other industries; they also favour creating more opportunities for farm workers to become smallholders and eventually small farmers."

Arch Bodley was not the only interviewee to have switched political parties to join the Liberals. The campaign also featured Ivar Campbell of Knowstone Manor, who explained why he had quit the Tories. He said: "The Conservative Party is dominated by powerful business interests. Time and again, these interests conflict with the needs of North Devon, and sometimes even with the needs of Britain itself. The Liberal MPs put their constituents and their country first. In Parliament, whether Conservatives or Labour are in power, the Liberals are a 'third force' for good, out of all proportion to their numbers."

The tactic of encouraging past Liberal voters and intending voters to express their opinions through media advertorials was tried again in 1963, as a Conservative party which had hit its peak in 1959 was faltering and Macmillan's image was badly tarnished. In addition to economic problems, the scandal involving Secretary of State for War John Profumo, who admitted having an affair with model Christine Keeler, who was alleged to have had a simultaneous relationship with a Soviet Union diplomat, creating a security risk, badly damaged the image of the government.

The 1963 North Devon Liberals' newspaper advertorial campaign was constructed around the slogan 'Look ahead with the Liberals'. Malcolm

Perkins, a bank employee, fastened on to the feeling, current among young people in 1963, when the first stirrings of the 'Swinging Sixties' were beginning to be felt, that the Conservative government was out of date and out of touch. Perkins said: "You don't have to be very old to realise that this country needs new and vigorous ideas to get it moving again along the right lines. So many young people are playing a leading part in building up the Liberal party these days that I feel quite at home."

Further evidence that the Liberals were successfully playing the youth card in North Devon was provided by Jean Brock, a member of the Young Liberals who lived in Chittlehampton, a party stronghold in the early '60s. She declared that the Liberal leader in 1963, Jo Grimond, had 'a lively mind and the sort of policies that appeal to everyone who wants to bring Britain up-to-date. She added: "The Liberal bid to end class divisions in politics and offer real opportunities to everyone appeals especially to young people. Socialists legislate to control us; Tories dither and pander to the few. I back the Liberals for a better future."

Perennial issues such as the cost of living, the plight of many pensioners and the future of farming in North Devon were also raised by contributors to the media campaign. Mrs F. J. Pope, a housewife and mother of four from Bideford said price rings and other forms of monopoly forced families to pay 'artificially high prices for so many things we buy in the shops'. She backed the Liberal plan to restore genuine competition that would bring these prices tumbling down and benefit everyone'.

The pensioner voice was represented by a Mr Hedger, who at the age of 85 in 1963 remembered the Liberals introducing the first old age pension in 1908. He added: "Today I know that here in North Devon, there is real hardship among many old people and that over the country as whole literally hundreds of thousands of pensioners draw National Assistance. The Liberal plan is to increase the pension, tie all pensions to the cost of living and abolish the earnings rule. I want to be represented by someone who minds about the welfare of the pensioner and will fight in Parliament for the old people."

Farmer Denys Smalldon resorted to grim irony when he commented: "Government farming policy has achieved the impossible. The subsidy bill has soared, food prices have continued to rise and real farm incomes have fallen. The Liberal policy aims at co-ordinating imports, improving marketing, cutting farmers' costs and making available cheap capital. That's why I, as a farmer, will be looking ahead with the Liberals."

Industrial relations, as ever, were high on the agenda of issues in 1963. Ken Hunt, a union activist from Barnstaple was surprised and irritated by people who believed that be a union member meant you had to be a socialist, adding: "There are many trades unionists who are Liberals, because they know it was the Liberals who gave us the right to have trades unions in the first place. What impresses me is that Jo Grimond is the only party leader who dares to say in public that the unions must bring themselves up to date. Labour won't because they get nearly all their money from them! It's because I respect and cherish trades union ideals that I want these reforms to take place."

Over the years the issues highlighted in the 1959 and 1963 media campaigns mirrored the questions being asked by Jeremy Thorpe in the House of Commons. Since his election he had campaigned vigorously on both local affairs and on the national and international issues that had been close to his heart from the moment he first became involved in student politics at Oxford – the future of the colonial remnants of the British Empire, apartheid, capital punishment, the United Nations and international relations in general.

Despite these wider concerns, and his growing reputation as a passionate and well-informed speaker on affairs in Africa and other parts of the developing world, his maiden speech squarely addressed the needs of North Devon, needs that were to run like a thread through his years as an MP.

The speech, delivered to the House on 10 November 1959, came during a debate on the government's local employment bill. He highlighted poor communications as the principal reason for the lack of employment opportunities in North Devon, and called for urgent government action. The command of language that was to ensure regular headlines for Thorpe was already to the fore as he told the House: "In my constituency the town of Ilfracombe in the summer enjoys great prosperity, but in the winter is faced with unemployment, which descends upon it like a disease."

He went on to highlight the broader West Country problem of lack of suitable and permanent jobs, summer and winter alike, for young people. "At the moment the cream of our youth is leaving the area because there is nothing for them. Of those unemployed in North Devon, 9% are under the age of 18."

Coinciding with the media campaign using actual voters to get across the message of Liberal policies, Jeremy Thorpe raged in 1963 on the subject of what had become one of his major themes – the need for positive methods to aid rural development. He bitterly criticised the refusal of a government loan to the Barnstaple firm of Shapland and Petter to safeguard jobs in Barnstaple, saying: "It is ironic that 450 people receiving unemployment assistance at approximately £6 per week would cost the government more than £140,000 a year.

"I was asking them to lend £125,000 [to Shapland and Petter], repayable by the company at current bank interest charges in order provide employment for those men. The loan was refused." Speaking on his own House of Commons motion, he urged the government to rectify the 'ridiculous imbalance' between rural and more developed areas by selecting four rural areas (including North Devon) into which they would 'deliberately and consciously pump red blood.'

In stark contrast to the Tories' travails during 1963, a revitalised Labour was fired with enthusiasm following Wilson's famous speech at the party's 1963 conference, when he argued that 'the Britain that is going to be forged in the white heat of this revolution will be no place for restrictive practices or for outdated measures on either side of industry' – a declaration that sealed Wilson's reputation as a technocrat not necessarily committed to the traditional class warfare traditions of the British left.

When in October 1964 the General Election to which the 1963 media campaign had formed a preliminary skirmish materialised, Thorpe returned to the issues he and his advisers had highlighted so effectively the year before. In his election address he admitted that the constituency still had real local problems to overcome. He said: "These issues are known to almost everyone; we suffer annually heavy seasonal unemployment and low wages; many small farmers are facing genuine economic hardship; the building of our new hospital has been pushed back three years; we badly need to bring some of our schools up to date – particularly primary schools;' two railway lines are threatened and a third is to be closed; our road speak for themselves."

On the stump throughout the constituency for the 1964 election, Jeremy Thorpe had accepted that progress on overcoming the problems of the West Country was often slow. One of the basic reasons for this lay in what would later be called a lack of critical mass. The region's predominantly Conservative MPs had, he claimed, collectively failed to work together to advance the interests of the area as a whole.

Thorpe went on to say: "Unless the West is repeatedly to be pushed to the bottom of the queue its Members of Parliament must hammer away again and again to make known our demands, whatever government is in power. One of my main criticisms of the West Country Conservative MPs is that they have failed to do this. A strong team of Liberal MPs would go to Westminster committed to fight for a new deal for the West."

During the 17 months of Harold Wilson's first premiership, Thorpe claimed the Liberals had done all they could to restrain a Labour administration with such a wafer-thin majority. Before the 1966 election he said the Liberal MPs, backed by the three million votes the party had secured in 1964, had exerted 'a dramatic influence' on the government. "We helped to kill the nationalisation of the steel industry and of building land. The first would have cost the electorate £650 million; the second would have increased the cost of house building. In addition, Liberal pressure persuaded the Labour administration to move modestly towards regionalisation.

Jeremy Thorpe continued throughout the 1960s and 1970s to spell out the basic priorities for ending the blight on North Devon. "We need not only more efficiency on the railways for factories but for what is our second largest industry; the holiday industry. Our roads are extremely bad and what is needed as much as more factories are better communications."

Like all politicians, he won on some issues and lost on others. He was unable to save the railway lines from Barnstaple to Taunton and from Barnstaple to Bideford and Torrington, but played a leading role in ensuring the survival of the Barnstaple to Exeter route. He also campaigned for better road communication with the outside world, which eventually materialised in the shape of the North Devon Link Road, opened in 1988, nine years after Thorpe had ceased to be an MP. Many people in North Devon believe that had he been around to be involved in the later stages of planning for the road, it would have been dual carriageway throughout.

Whilst campaigning for the conditions which would attract manufacturing and service industries to North Devon, Thorpe never forgot the constituency's traditional core industry of agriculture and his grasp of the problems faced by farmers is still remembered today.

Roger Dapling has farmed in the West Country since 1947 and in that time has seen half a dozen Members of Parliament and countless aspiring but unsuccessful candidates come and go. In his opinion no one over those seven decades measures up to Jeremy Thorpe. "He was good for North Devon," is Roger's simple summing-up.

Although Roger and his wife Anne, like the majority of North Devonians, first encountered Thorpe when he was canvassing in the constituency, Roger had a closer view of how the MP operated. As a member of delegations from the local branch of the National Farmers Union, he attended meetings at Thorpe's cottage at Higher Chuggaton, with the MP opening his home to representatives of the industry.

Roger and Anne farmed first at Ilkerton, near Lynton and later at Pinkery, just across the border in West Somerset, and then returned to North Devon at The Barton, Kentisbury. Roger recalls: "Jeremy was helpful to the NFU. He seemed to be able to slot right in and understand the problems faced by farmers. He was always well briefed about the agricultural world and came out with a lot of good ideas. He achieved a great deal for North Devon and I don't think that will ever be forgotten."

Jeremy Thorpe's wit and sense of mischief rubbed off on others. One local government representative from a particularly rural part of North Devon, who preferred not to be identified, summed up a factor in his appeal to those who worked the land. "The farmers liked him. The fact that he was a bit flashy in his appearance was in his favour as far as they were concerned – he reminded them of the auctioneers in the livestock markets."

9. Jeremy and his Opponents

The Parliamentary friendships that develop between individual members, whose politics and party affiliations are poles apart, never cease to amaze the ordinary voter, whose visual image of politicians, greatly enhanced since the televising of debates, is based on the bickering, denunciations and insults that fly across the floor of the House of Commons.

A prime example of the realities of life for MPs, both inside and outside the debating chamber and committee rooms at Westminster, occurred in the early months of 1967, shortly after Jeremy Thorpe's election as leader of the Parliamentary Liberal party. A considerable contributory part of the enduring Thorpe legend suggests that he was popular not just among Liberal members and supporters, nationally and in North Devon, but was generally well liked too by his opponents. The 1967 incident and other available evidence suggests that this popularity was considerably more than a myth.

Shortly after the Liberal leadership election, North Devon-based photographers Marcus and Denzil Bath were summoned to Taunton Railway Station to photograph the triumphant return of the new leader to the West Country. Waiting on the platform were a group of Liberal officials from North Devon, who planned to travel from Taunton to Barnstaple through villages in Jeremy Thorpe's constituency, stopping to greet party members along the route.

When the photographs had been taken to Thorpe's satisfaction, he surprised and gratified the Bath brothers by inviting them to join the party for refreshments at what was then Taunton's premier hotel, The County, an impressive building on East Street, which today no longer fulfils its original function. After the group had settled around a table in the hotel, Thorpe scanned the dining room and leapt to his feet when he spotted a familiar face, that of Peter Mills, the Conservative MP for North Devon's neighbouring constituency of Torrington (now Torridge).

Marcus Bath recalls: "Jeremy bounded across the room in his usual flamboyant manner, held out his arms and said: Peter, how nice to see you. Surely you are not going to lunch alone. Come across and join us at my table." Back at Jeremy's table, eyebrows were being raised and, as Marcus Bath remembers: "There was a sudden feeling of tension. Surely the new leader of the Liberal Party was not going to be seen eating in public with a Tory MP! I don't think any of us realised until that day that this sort of thing was the norm in Parliament, which after all has been described as London's finest Gentleman's Club. It was certainly a lesson to us about how politicians actually lived, and a demonstration of how outgoing Jeremy Thorpe really was. I have certainly never forgotten the incident."

Jeremy Thorpe's cordial relationships with political opponents are fairly well documented in the considerable body of literature that concerns the

Liberal party leader and have lingered in the memories of those who came close to him at the time. What has also been well covered is the fact that many of Thorpe's opponents perhaps had a better opinion of the man than some of his colleagues within his own party. In fact, anyone reading accounts of his career might well come to the conclusion that some of his worst enemies were to be found not among the ranks of the Conservatives and Labour, but among his Parliamentary Liberal party colleagues.

The 1967 leadership election (covered earlier in Chapter 4 Ambition Fulfilled: Thorpe as Liberal Leader) was controversial in as much as it was seen by many to be unduly rushed through and could be said to be unrepresentative of the Liberal Party as a whole, given that the Liberal MPs, 12 in number at the time, formed the entire electorate.

The election, although a victory for Thorpe, was by no means a win by general acclamation and, perhaps understandably given the nature of politics, there were to be regular mutterings and the odd plot throughout Jeremy's nine-year-tenure of the post.

Recriminations were far from the mind of those present in Taunton that day, and after the meal a cavalcade of cars, headed by Thorpe himself in his Sunbeam Talbot, set off for the boundary of the North Devon constituency. From that point on until Barnstaple was reached it was a succession of lightning stops, cheers, much sounding of car horns, a brief speech from the leader and off again along the old A361 road.

The main opponents for Jeremy Thorpe in his eight electoral contests within North Devon – unlike many aspiring politicians in all the main parties he never contested any other Parliamentary seat – were the Conservatives, despite the shock General Election result of 1951 when the Liberals in the division had been pushed into third place by Labour.

Thorpe's first Tory opponent, in 1955, after Jeremy had nursed the seat for the three years since his adoption as Liberal candidate in 1952, was James Lindsay, whose impact on the constituency was somewhat limited. Like Thorpe, Lindsay came from a political family and was elected to Parliament at the same time as a nephew. He was the second and youngest son of David Lindsay, 27th Earl of Crawford and, again like Thorpe, was educated at Eton and Oxford University. He fought in World War Two as a major in the King's Royal Rifle Corps.

Lindsay took the seat in 1955 but when the two men went head to head for the second time in 1959, Thorpe overturned Lindsay's majority of more than 5,000, to be returned by 362 votes. After his one term in the House of Commons, Lindsay vanished from the political scene. In the run-up to the 1959 contest Lindsay was given something of a roasting in the columns of the *News Chronicle*, a newspaper which admittedly supported the Liberal Party.

From time immemorial newspapers have despatched their special correspondents to constituencies at General Election times to gather gossip and write 'colour' stories to liven up election coverage which otherwise could degenerate into rather dull debates on policies which generally fail to excite the average voter. The *Chronicle*, which in 1959 had little more than a year of its 78-

year existence before being swallowed up by its Tory rival the *Daily Mail*, is perhaps best remembered today by those of a certain age as being the home of the popular I-Spy column, which was supplemented by a series of little books which enabled young people to answer questions about things they saw whilst travelling around the country.

The reporter sent to North Devon from the *Chronicle's* Bouverie Street (off Fleet Street) home was Joyce Eggington, who damned Lindsay in the first sentence of her article, part of a series reviewing Liberal party prospects in the West Country. Eggington wrote: "It says much for North Devon conservatism – with a small *c* – that James Lindsay has been local Tory MP for four years and is still regarded as a stranger in his own constituency, having made the mistake of once farming in Somerset."

She went on to say: "It says much for North Devon contrariness that of the three men who will contest the election, the only one who was born in the area – Labour's prospective candidate Geoffrey Pitt – is least likely to win."

The *Chronicle* piece is useful for the snapshot it gives of North Devon preparing for the General Election that was to launch the Westminster career of Jeremy Thorpe, whose years representing the seat gave the area a profile it had never previously experienced and may well never know again. It was a time of rising prosperity in Britain (at least on the surface) and a time when not only thousands of holidaymakers flocked annually into North Devon but also an increasing tide of those seeking to make the area their permanent home.

The *News Chonicle's* Eggington reported that all three political parties considered they had something to gain from the influx of newcomers. The Conservatives claimed more than a thousand new members enrolled in the past year whilst the Liberals had increased their active branches in the towns and villages of the constituency from six to 32. Labour, for its part, was convinced that it had many new supporters among the 'foreigners', who included many elderly Midlanders and Londoners retiring to the West Country, hoping to settle in comfort, augmenting their pensions with light part-time jobs. The fly in the ointment – and it is a familiar fly where North Devon is concerned – was then and now the shortage of such jobs.

James Lindsay was described in the *Chronicle* article as 'lacking the Peto attraction' – a reference to the father and son duo who had represented the Barnstaple and later the North Devon division for spells in the 1920s, 1930s, 1940s and 1950s. Lindsay, said Joyce Eggington, was "conscientious but shy. He avoids publicity and his voice is seldom heard in the Commons. That is a loss, since North Devonians love a good talker. Mr Lindsay's appeal could be summed up in words used by a Barnstaple waitress when I asked what was in a certain dish: 'it's a kind of mixture really. Quite all right if you like that kind of thing.'"

In contrast, Jeremy Thorpe was described in the *Chronicle* as a foreigner who has steadily acquired Devon nationality. "The personal touch counts for a lot in North Devon, a point proved by the Peto family. If the Liberals need it, this gives them extra confidence in the go-ahead Mr Thorpe. People in North Devon consider themselves lucky that he holds several high offices in the

Liberal Party and – a piquant touch they love to quote – his father and grandfather were both Tory MPs." Joyce Eggington concluded: "Add all those views and you have a fair picture of the pride and prejudices of North Devon political thought," she added.

The *News Chronicle* journalist's reference to the Peto family and the influence of the personal touch in North Devon politics spotlighted the only dynasty to feature in the history of the Barnstaple and North Devon Parliamentary constituencies. The Peto name re-appeared for the 1964 General Election, Jeremy Thorpe's first defence of the seat he had won in 1959. This time the family was represented by another Basil Peto, son of Chrisopher Peto and grandson of the earlier MP and his namesake. As it was, the re-acquaintance of the Peto family with North Devon politics was to be brief, as Thorpe won the seat with a comfortable majority of more than 5,000.

Thorpe's next two Conservative opponents were both Devonians and both veered towards the right wing of the party. First up, to take on Thorpe at the 1966 General Election, was Timothy Carleton Keigwin, who was to become the nearly man of politics in the constituency. Keigwin was a farmer from West Anstey and, like the two senior members of the Peto dynasty, had a distinguished war record, having been awarded the Military Cross (MC) in 1944, whilst serving as a Lieutenant with the 1st Battalion Irish Guards in Italy.

Twice Keigwin pulled off creditable General Election results against Jeremy Thorpe, on the second occasion coming close to causing a sensation. Standing for the first time in 1966, Keigwin reduced Thorpe's majority from the 5,136 recorded in 1964 to 1,166. The 1970 General Election, Thorpe's first as party leader, came perilously close to being a disaster. When the result was announced Thorpe had squeezed home by just 369 votes.

There was not to be a third time lucky for Keigwin; the local man held on as candidate until the first General Election of 1974, held in the February of that year, with the North Devon constituency, as a result of boundary changes, now including the Borough of Bideford and the surrounding rural areas. Jeremy Thorpe received a thumping 34,000 votes to Keigwin's total of just under 23,000. The Liberal leader's majority was 11,000 plus. Keigwin, who had been active politically outside the General Election hustings, as a member of the controversial Monday Club, which supported the illegal Ian Smith regime in Rhodesia (now Zimbabwe) and took a tough line on immigration, retired from the fray, with the consolation that, several years later, he became High Sheriff of the County of Devon.

Keigwin's published comments after his decision to stand aside reveal his considerable bitterness about the state of British politics in the mid-1970s, stemming from his belief that every seat held or gained by the Liberals was helping to put Labour and their trade union allies in power. His unsuccessful campaign had constantly reiterated this message, in strong language, summed up by his claim in the press that, if by voting Liberal, "you create a situation of weakness which allows Britain to be taken over by the Marxists, you will bitterly regret it. The situation is too serious for side issues or splinter parties."

The huge Thorpe majority in February 1974 brought forth what was described as a blistering attack from Keigwin against what he described as 'television gimmicks and press hysteria'. The General Election result, producing a minority Labour government meant, he said, that the country was 'drifting, leaderless, gutless and pathetic, on to the rocks'. His farewell message to North Devon's electorate concluded: "I wish you all the best of luck in the dangerous days that lie ahead, and I have no doubt that we are all going to need it."

The Labour candidate in February 1974, Terry Marston (who lost his deposit), was little happier than Tim Keigwin. In his case he deplored the fact that many would-be Labour voters had cast their vote for the Liberals in an attempt to prevent a Tory being elected in North Devon, adding: "We now see the result generally of this type of negative voting which has plunged the country into the uncertainty of a minority government at such a critical time. Countless Tories have slipped in through Liberal intervention which has had the effect of undermining Labour as the only possible Parliamentary alternative to the Tories."

With Keigwin retired from the fray, the mantle of trying to regain the North Devon division for the Tories now fell to Tony Speller, an Exeter-born businessman who as a national service man had helped with rescue work in Lynmouth at the time of the 1952 flood disaster in the Exmoor seaside resort. Though considered to be on the right of the Conservative party, he had strong views on environmental issues and was an opponent of the Poll Tax, the issue which was one of the factors that led to the eventual demise of Margaret Thatcher. He was, as we have seen, ultimately successful in 1979 and retained the seat for 13 years.

The Labour Party has never been a strong force in North Devon politics. The traditional essentials for Labour strength, a mass working class vote and a strong base of trades unionism have never existed in the constituency. The first candidate to stand for the then Barnstaple division was Richard Gifford in 1923, who trailed in third with just 1,225 votes, behind the victorious Liberal, Tudor Rees with 14,880 and the Unionist Basil Peto, with 13,614. Labour only contested the seat once at the four General Elections up until 1945. In that contest the party polled more than 10,000 votes, a record result until 1951, when a strong local candidate, Bill Wilkey, a one-time Mayor of Barnstaple, created a sensation by beating the Liberals into third place. Wilkey's 10,632 votes remains a Labour record for North Devon.

One of the few survivors among the ranks of those who opposed Jeremy Thorpe over the years, and the only opponent to go on to have a successful political career, is Chris Mullin, who recounted his very positive recollections of Thorpe in his immensely readable memoir, *Hinterland*. In the book Mullin's self-deprecating comment on his experiences in North Devon in 1970 are summed up when he says: "At the grand old age of 22 I was far too young and immature to represent anyone!"

At university Mullin, who went on to hold ministerial position in Labour governments, studied law but found himself spending more time working for the student newspaper than studying his subject and decided to become a journalist instead – a move which brought him to the West Country. He joined the Mirror Group training scheme, originally being rejected but gaining a last minute place when another candidate dropped out.

The scheme was based around a group of local newspapers in South Devon and in years to come prominent graduates from the scheme would include Alastair Campbell (destined to become a key player in the rise of New Labour), Andrew Morton (whose works include *Diana: Her True Story*) and David Montgomery, who went on to edit the *News of the World* and later became chief executive of the Mirror Group.

Mullin explains: "The idea was that, after a course in the basics of journalism, we would be apprenticed to one or more of the half dozen weekly newspapers owned by the group. I must have been particularly insufferable because I ended up being shunted around all six!

Whilst still a trainee journalist, he was selected as the Labour candidate for North Devon at the 1970 General Election. "There was not the slightest danger of being called upon to represent anyone, even if I had been fit to do. Even in those days Labour voters in the constituency numbered little more than 5,000. The sitting MP, clinging on by his fingertips against a strong Conservative challenge, was the Liberal Leader Jeremy Thorpe.

"Thorpe impressed me for several reasons. North Devon was a classic rural seat. Most of his constituents were opposed to what was then known as the Common Market; he was in favour. They were strongly anti-immigrant (there were virtually no foreigners in North Devon at that time) but he was liberal on immigration. Most of his constituents were keen on the death penalty though murders in North Devon were rare; he was opposed."

It was not just Thorpe's ability to carry with him voters who were generally opposed to his political views that impressed Mullin, but his solicitude for a younger opponent starting out on a political career. "At the election count, when I was found to be a few votes short of holding on to my deposit (which in those days required 12.5 per cent of the total votes cast rather than the present 5 per cent) he graciously insisted on a recount, to see if the extra votes could be found.

"In those days, before misfortune overtook him, Thorpe had galvanised political life in North Devon, holding meetings in every village, sometimes as many as four or five a night, in addition to his gruelling schedule of national events. The electoral turnout was 85 per cent and a crowd of several thousand attended the final hustings and the declaration of the result. Much of that was down to his extraordinary magnetism. I might have been young and impressionable, but I remember Jeremy Thorpe as I saw him when he was at the height of his powers, rather than the tragic figure he later became."

Mullin eventually won the Sunderland South Parliamentary constituency, which he represented from 1987 to 2010. In the 1980s he made a great reputation for himself as an investigative journalist, leading a campaign that resulted in the release of the Birmingham Six, victims of a miscarriage of justice. He was also the author of the novel *A Very British Coup* which was later adapted for television and was editor of the *Tribune* newspaper from 1982–84, where he provided effective support for Tony Benn.

He was appointed as Parliamentary Under-Secretary of State at the DETR in July 1999 before taking over from George Foulkes as Parliamentary Under-Secretary, Department for International Development in 2001. He returned to government in June 2003, as a Parliamentary Under-Secretary at the Foreign Office, but after the 2005 election again returned to the backbenches.

Before the Labour victory of 1997, Mullin had attained a reputation for campaigning on behalf of victims of injustice. His campaigning stance had to change while a minister because of the collective responsibility of government. His vote against the government's proposal for 90 days' detention without trial for terrorist suspects, as one of 49 Labour rebels concerned seemed to indicate a re-emergence of his civil libertarian instincts. He criticised the Labour government's commitment to its expressed policy on Africa. During the UK Parliamentary expenses scandal Mullin, one of the lowest claimers, provided comic relief when it was revealed that the television at his second home was a very old black-and-white model. He stood down from Parliament at the 2010 general election.

Jeremy Thorpe's relationship with Harold Wilson, the man who led the Labour party for much of Thorpe's time in Parliament, has been the subject of considerable speculation over the years. When Wilson died in May 1995 Thorpe paid tribute to a man he described as 'a good friend and a formidable opponent', adding: "He was a great Parliamentarian and a dedicated democrat. His belief in democracy was not limited to fine phrases but led to positive action."

Despite their very different backgrounds, Old Etonian Thorpe's Kensington and Knightsbridge roots and Wilson's upbringing in industrial West Yorkshire and Cheshire, where he attended council school and later grammar schools, the two men's career paths merged at Oxford. Wilson, several years ahead of Thorpe at the University, was an officer of the Oxford University Liberal Club before turning to Labour; Wilson's father's politics had originally been Liberal.

The distinguished biographer Ben Pimlott, in his scholarly but immensely readable biography of Harold Wilson, describes the Labour Prime Minister's political beliefs as espousing a 'Lib-Lab, nonconformist, free-thinking egalatarianism' and the first two factors at least were still to the forefront in the Liberal party when led by Thorpe.

Towards the end of his Premiership, Harold Wilson suspected that, as a long-time opponent of apartheid in Southern Africa, he had been targeted by South African agents. Jeremy Thorpe too had a track record in opposing the regimes in Rhodesia and South Africa and, in 1976 Wilson, in Pimlott's words, "rushed to the defence of Thorpe, suggesting in a meeting that the Norman Scott allegations against the Liberal leader might have been exploited by the South Africans."

One of the landmark occasions in the history of Labour politics in North Devon was surely the occasion in the spring of 1962 when Wilson, the party leader, paid a visit to the constituency party. In contrast to a visit to the constituency made by a prominent Conservative cabinet minister, who failed to observe the usual courtesy of informing Thorpe as the local MP of his intentions, Wilson approached Jeremy about his trip, insisting that he would not be dealing with the Liberals but would concentrate in his speech on attacking the record of the Tory government.

In his autobiography, *In My Own Time*, Thorpe includes an amusing anecdote about the Wilson excursion into North Devon. Jeremy suggested to Wilson that as he was travelling to his seat on the same date, he would be pleased to give the Labour leader a lift across Exmoor from Taunton railway station. Wilson asked Thorpe if his supporters would object, with Jeremy replying, "I doubt it, but if they do, I shall tell them that an opponent should not be treated as a mortal enemy."

During the car journey Thorpe gave Wilson a briefing on what he should expect of the Labour movement in North Devon. The party's strength lay in pockets, the candidate at the next election should expect to lose his deposit (he duly did), there would be an attendance at Wilson's meeting of between 15 and 20 people, the chairman of the meeting would be a former Liberal converted to socialism. Thorpe's final thrust was to assure Wilson that no arrangements would be made to feed him, so he would be expected to return to Thorpe's current home for a late supper.

En route to Barnstaple Thorpe's car rounded a sharp bend on a narrow lane to be confronted by a broken down wagon loaded with hay bales blocking the way, with the farmer frantically moving the bales into a field. According to Thorpe's account, Wilson said, in a jocular manner, "I suppose this has been laid on", with Thorpe's reply being, "Yes, this is an ambush by the North Devon savages."

Getting Wilson to his meeting on time was a point of honour for Thorpe and it was suggested that he and his guest should turn to and help the farmer. Wilson agreed, rolled up his sleeves and set to work. The farmer recognised Jeremy Thorpe but continued to look quizzically at Wilson, until Thorpe made the necessary introduction, explaining that the Labour leader had very kindly come down to North Devon to help with the hay harvest. The farmer's reply was to the point; "very kind, I'm sure!"

Harold Wilson made the meeting on time, although the Labour faithful were astonished to see their speaker driven to the door by the local Liberal MP. Wilson got out of Thorpe's car, with wisps of hay still clinging to him and, as Jeremy described it, with total aplomb went into the meeting. Thorpe's telling of the tale ended in the following fashion: "Later that evening a Labour supporter brought Harold to the country hotel where I was living. Harold told me that the meeting was as I had prophesied, likewise the likely outcome in the next General Election and, most importantly, the absence of supper. This was soon repaired."

Relationships with local government opponents in North Devon could prove just as cordial and mutually productive.

One of the longest-serving and most respected local government representatives in North Devon is Raymond Liverton, whose many years of service to the community was marked by his appointment as an Honorary Alderman following his retirement from North Devon Council.

His political memories in North Devon go back more than 80 years, to the time when he and other children marched up and down Station Hill in the village Swimbridge in the run-up to the 1935 General Election, holding candles in jam jars and chanting 'Vote, Vote, Vote for Dicky Ackland', in support of the Liberal candidate.

Ray, who also chaired the Parish Council in Swimbridge for many years, is proud of the fact that during his years as a district councillor, he never accepted a penny in expenses or allowances. He is a lifelong Conservative (although standing for the council as an Independent) but is vehement in his praise of Jeremy Thorpe as an MP.

"Jeremy Thorpe, in my opinion, was the finest MP this constituency has ever had, or ever will have," he says. "Whenever I had a problem in the ward I represented I knew I could contact Jeremy and he would respond and do his best to help find a solution."

Alec Pickersgill, Conservative agent in the latter years of Thorpe's time as MP, sums up the position of a great many North Devon voters. "When I first arrived in North Devon it was common for people who regarded themselves as Conservative supporters to confess that what they really wanted was a Conservative Government at Westminster but with Jeremy Thorpe re-elected as the MP for North Devon.

"North Devonians not only fell for Thorpe's charm but they were highly susceptible to his high profile as a national politician. The area is often depicted as something of a backwater and they liked seeing their MP reflected back at them on television. They also liked the fact that his father and his grandfather had been Conservative MPs and that his mother was a Conservative activist.

"It made many people feel they could vote for Jeremy without compromising their Conservative principles."

10. A Devoted Liberal to His Last Breath

Jeremy Thorpe's attempts to re-enter public life were doomed to failure. He was nevertheless able to draw some consolation from the knowledge that his years of service were recognised from time to time, to a limited and some would say rather grudging extent within the national party and, with considerably more enthusiasm and sense of gratitude within the Parliamentary constituency he had represented so well and for so long.

A number of diehards within the Liberal ranks in North Devon, encouraged by occasional media speculation about Thorpe's possible return to active politics, continued to dream of a triumphant comeback with Jeremy, in their estimation, the man best situated to win back the now Conservative-held constituency.

His closest associates within both the national and local parties took a more realistic view, setting their sights no higher than doing their best to ensure that Thorpe was not allowed to believe he had been completely forgotten.

It took a little time after the events of 1979 for the local association to come together to honour their former MP. They gathered in July 1981 at the North Devon Motel in Barnstaple to make a presentation to Jeremy. The main gift was a large watercolour collage, with his own cottage, Higher Chuggaton near Cobbaton (at that time part of the widespread parish of Swimbridge), as the centrepiece, surrounded by 15 cameos of North Devon scenes. The collage was the work of a talented local artist, John Dyke, who was particularly noted as the designer of many of the stamps issued by Lundy Island. The choice of artist was fitting, given Thorpe's own role in helping to save Lundy for the nation.

Harold Richardson, President of the North Devon Liberal Association and John Gregory, the Chairman, also presented Jeremy with what was described as an 'elaborate' record player. A third item, an ornamental wooden arch bridge, had already been erected across the duck pond in the grounds of the Cobbaton cottage. The fund launched by the Liberal Association for the purpose raised £1,500.

Such was the continuing interest in Thorpe's activities that Liberal agent Peter Bray needed to assure the national media that there was nothing 'strange or sinister' about the delay in recognising the former MP's contribution, saying: "You don't paint a picture or build a bridge overnight. So we needed time to get everything ship-shape."

Bray forcefully dismissed the continuing flow of media revelations about what was claimed to be the 'real truth` about the Norman Scott affair and scorned suggestions of a political comeback. He said: "No one here is influenced by any new revelations concerning Jeremy. We have always stood by him. There is no local gossip about him wanting to get back into Parliament –

we've had enough of gossip. Jeremy is now just a normal local party member."

Lilian Prowse did not long continue to drive the North Devon association once Jeremy Thorpe had retired from the scene. She gave up most of her responsibilities in the summer of 1980, having spent her final months at the helm assisting the new Liberal candidate, Roger Blackmore to settle into the constituency and face the gargantuan task of succeeding such a towering personality.

There was again something of a delay before Lilian's services were recognised by the presentation of framed prints. The occasion reunited former MP and his long-time agent, with Jeremy Thorpe present alongside his successor Roger Blackmore in a display of party unity. Speaking at the ceremony Jeremy said: "It is difficult to express my admiration, gratitude and affection for her, we had a political partnership lasting 20 years. And if ever there was a disagreement, she was usually right.

"I came to rely on her as a loyal, devoted and wise companion. If we had been lucky enough to have a dozen people like Lilian Prowse in the 1950s and 1960s, the whole of British politics would have been transformed. She was like a second Member of Parliament; LP in North Devon meant either the Liberal Party or Lilian Prowse."

Roger Blackmore, whose attempts to regain the seat for the party were unsuccessful, acknowledged the reputation Lilian Prowse enjoyed within the political world, saying: "She was probably the finest political agent of her time in any party. When she started, the Liberal party was laughed at. Plenty of us said things should be changed, but Lilian taught us that it could be done.

"She never believed that she had to be swept along with the current; that's a lesson she has bequeathed to a whole generation. Another lesson she taught us was that you can have superb ideas and dreams to better mankind, but it comes to nothing unless you have determination, drive and the organisation to make it a reality."

Mrs Prowse told the party faithful at the gathering: "We have come a long way together since I first became active in the 1950s." Taking advantage of the occasion to pay her own tribute to Thorpe she added: "Thank you Jeremy for the appreciation, fun and excitement of working together to turn North Devon into Liberal country."

In 1987 the status of 'just a normal party member' was amended when Jeremy Thorpe was appointed President of the Constituency Liberal (later Liberal Democrat) Association. The position was far from being honorary; Nick Harvey (who regained North Devon for the Liberals in 1992, capturing the constituency from Tony Speller after it had been for 13 years in Conservative hands) recalled in later years: "Jeremy never lost his razor sharp mind, his amazing memory, his passion for politics or his sense of mischief. As President of the Association he was a great support to me as a young candidate aiming to win back the seat.

"He was a source of advice, encouragement, one-liners, fund-raising drives – not to mention a few mad-cap ideas."

An event which marked a melting of the frigidity which had been a hallmark of the Liberal party's treatment of Jeremy Thorpe came in April 2009, described by the journalist David Randall as 'an absolution of sorts'. A party to mark Thorpe's 80th birthday was held at the National Liberal Club.

His final public appearance was also in 2009, at the unveiling of a bust of himself in the Grimond Room at the House of Commons, by which time both Jeremy and Marion were in wheelchairs. Jeremy's pleasure at a further act of recognition was enhanced by the presence at the ceremony of Liberal Democrat leader Nick Clegg and former leaders, David Steel, Menzies Campbell and Charles Kennedy, together with members of the Grimond and Bonham Carter families. When the Speaker of the House of Commons, John Bercow, via his Advisory Committee on Works of Art, realised that no portrait or bust of Jeremy Thorpe was held in the Parliamentary Collection, the Thorpe family was approached and agreed that a new cast could be taken from an existing bust in their possession.

The original bust had been sculpted by Avril Vellacott, an artist with North Devon connections, who at the unveiling ceremony recalled her encounters with the former Liberal leader whilst working on the likeness. She said at the time "I found Jeremy Thorpe an excellent sitter; he had the ideal face for portrait sculpture because of his fine bone structure. He sat for me in his office at the Commons, and as I worked I was amused by the regular, and strident, interruptions from Big Ben. It was a great honour for me to be asked to sculpt him. As my local Member of Parliament for North Devon and as Leader of the Liberal party he was greatly respected. I feel similarly honoured now that this piece joins the Parliamentary Art Collection."

Hugo Swire MP, chairman of the Speaker's Advisory Committee on Works of Art said: "We are delighted that Jeremy Thorpe will now be represented in the Collection. As the Leader of the Liberal party, he combined youthful exuberance with a brilliant mind and made a significant contribution to British politics during the turbulent years of the 1960s and '70s. We added portraits busts of Harold Wilson and Ted Heath some time ago, so it is entirely right that Jeremy Thorpe should now take his place in history beside them."

Nick Clegg and John Bercow both spoke at the ceremony. Clegg recalled a recent encounter with a couple from Devon who complained of the 'sameness and ordinariness' of current politicians, who they said lacked depth, flair and imagination, quite unlike Jeremy Thorpe in his heyday. Clegg added that Thorpe's contribution to Liberal history ought to be judged by the difference in the vote achieved by the party at the general election of 1970, when just over two million votes were polled, and the general election of February 1974, when the tally went up to more than six million. "That leap in support was a testament to Jeremy Thorpe's political talent and his leadership of the Liberal Party," he said.

Speaker Bercow said Jeremy Thorpe had a wit and eloquence that could charm even opponents; when he spoke in the House of Commons the chamber filled up. Bercow added: "Jeremy Thorpe was a progressive in an age that was less progressive than it is today."

Jeremy himself, to the surprise of some of the guests at the ceremony, responded, making a particular point about the 'enormous debt of gratitude' he owed to his wife Marion for all her love, help and support over the years and to members of his family as well as to friends and colleagues in the Liberal Party and the Liberal Democrats.

Marion Thorpe died on 6 March 2014; Jeremy survived her by barely nine months, dying on 4 December of that same year. The Liberal Democratic Party hierarchy was present again at his funeral, at St Margaret's, Westminster on 17 December. The congregation on this occasion included all five of the leaders of the Liberals and Liberal Democrats who succeeded Thorpe – David Steel, Paddy Ashdown, Charles Kennedy, Menzies Campbell and Nick Clegg.

Fittingly, despite the presence of those who had led the party, it was Nick Harvey, the man who won back Thorpe's beloved constituency of North Devon, who paid the main tribute to his illustrious predecessor. Harvey acknowledged the presence of the leadership as he spoke about Thorpe's "devotion to the Liberal cause – sustained to his last breath."

There was nevertheless something for the assembled great and good of the party to ponder as they made their way home from the funeral and the gathering that followed at the National Liberal Club. Harvey said: "It was (Jeremy Thorpe's) unending sadness, and that of many friends that – despite time being the great healer – the party never quite found it in its heart to forgive or re-embrace its prodigal son, preferring to airbrush him out of its history, But it would have meant a great deal to him that all his successors as leader are here today, and that his contribution to the Liberal revival had been acknowledged. He will be fondly remembered and greatly missed."

In his address Nick Harvey paid tribute to Jeremy Thorpe's achievements in his constituency, in national politics, and in the international sphere. In the case of North Devon, he coupled Thorpe's name with that of Lilian Prowse, saying: "Between them they revived the historic Liberal tradition".

For the Liberals nationally, with his 'wit, zeal and panache', Jeremy as a new MP was the personification of hope when it was needed most. Harvey went on to say: "If Jo Grimond gave re-birth to the Liberal party's intellectual self-confidence and defined the Liberal creed for a new era, Jeremy, who succeeded him as leader in 1967 – gave re-birth to its campaigning self-confidence, turning it into a truly national force once again.

His Liberal successor as North Devon MP recalled Thorpe's 'fierce and unwavering' commitment to Liberal principles', adding: "As the son and grandson of leading Conservative MPs and the product of Eton and Oxford, the Conservative career ladder beckoned.

"But Jeremy was no Conservative. He wore it as a badge of honour that he was banned from Franco's Spain; his suggestion to bomb Ian Smith's railway supply lines in renegade Rhodesia caused great controversy; he was an impassioned anti-Apartheid campaigner before it became fashionable. He was a trenchant pro-European and campaigned alongside Ted Heath and Roy Jenkins in the 1975 Referendum campaign, with the trip packing 4,000 into Barnstaple's Pannier Market for a momentous rally."

With diplomatic representatives from African nations present at the funeral,

Nick Harvey recalled Jeremy Thorpe's championship of the continent. "He befriended President Kenneth Kaunda of Zambia and many other African leaders. Even in his later years he was writing to international leaders urging them to adopt post-Apartheid South African townships and help them rebuild and develop."

On a lighter note Harvey recalled Jeremy Thorpe's powers of mimicry and his ability to respond to hecklers with imitations of their own voices; "he could mock people *and* win their vote." Friends were not immune from the mimicry. "Jeremy would ring the Bonham Carters and other political families, brilliantly impersonating their relatives and causing absolute mischief. His astonishing memory for faces and names enabled him to boom loud greetings to people in the streets and markets, to their lasting delight and the envy of their friends.

"An entire generation of ladies took him to their hearts; he was mothered to distraction and I have come acress several men, now in their late forties, named Jeremy in his honour!"

*At the time of Jeremy Thorpe's funeral Nick Harvey was still the Member of Parliament for North Devon and the Liberal Party was a partner with David Cameron's Conservatives in a formal Coalition Government (2010-2015) – something Jeremy Thorpe had dreamt of but never achieved. Harvey achieved ministerial status as Minister of State for the Armed Forces in the Coalition between 2010 and 2012. He was knighted after leaving the ministerial post in a government re-shuffle. He lost his seat in the General Election 2015 by 6,936 votes. He contested the seat unsuccessfully in the General Election 2017, increasing his vote by 8.6%, but falling 4,332 votes short. In 2017 Sir Nick was appointed as chief executive of the Liberal Democratic party.

Appendix i
Jeremy Thorpe's North Devon Election Campaigns

Jeremy Thorpe, first selected as prospective Liberal parliamentary candidate for North Devon in 1952, fought eight General Election campaigns in the constituency. He lost his first contest in 1955, won the seat in 1959, and retained it on five occasions, in 1964, 1966, 1970, 1974 (February) and 1974 (October). He lost the seat in 1979, just before standing trial at the Old Bailey. He was acquitted on all charges but never returned to political life.

General Election 1955. This was Jeremy Thorpe's first parliamentary election campaign, fought after he had nursed the constituency for nearly three years. Nationally Labour had won a landslide victory in the 1945 General Election but in 1950 could only win a slim majority of five seats. This administration lasted for just 20 months and when the country went to the polls again in 1951 the Tories, with their National Liberal allies, secured 321 seats, with an overall majority of 17. This election marked the beginning of the Labour party's thirteen-year spell in opposition, and the return of Winston Churchill as Prime Minister. Jeremy Thorpe restored Liberal honour and helped to erase memories of the 1951 poll, when the party's candidate had been forced into a humiliating third place. Thorpe increased the Liberal's share of the vote from 19.41 per cent in 1951 to a much healthier 32.45 per cent, although he could not prevent the Conservative candidate, James Lindsay, from being returned, he saw the winner's majority cut by nearly 4,000.

Result:
James Lindsay (Conservative) 16,784
Jeremy Thorpe (Liberal) 11,558
Harold Heslop (Labour) 7,272
Majority 5,226

General Election 1959. Jeremy Thorpe's first electoral triumph in North Devon proved to be the only seat won by the Liberal Party at the poll. Having lost one of its existing seats, the party went into the new parliament with just six seats. Thorpe's victory over the Conservative sitting member, albeit by a wafer thin majority of 362 votes, nevertheless encouraged the Liberal party both nationally and in North Devon, where it had built up its strength on the ground in the constituency. Nationally Harold Macmillan cemented his hold on Number 10 Downing Street, with a Commons majority of 101 seats.

Result:
Jeremy Thorpe (Liberal) 15,831
James Lindsay (Conservative 15,649
Geoffrey Pitt (Labour) 5,567
Majority: 362

General Election 1964. Jeremy Thorpe boosted his tiny majority of 364 to a comfortable 5,136, recording more than 50 per cent of the total vote. The Conservatives fielded Basil Peto a futher member of a family that had previously held the Barnstaple and North Devon seats for the Conservatives. Nationally Labour, under Harold Wilson, won a tiny overall majority of just four seats against Conservatives led by Sir Alec Douglas-Home, who had succeeded Harold Macmillan. The Liberals, led by Jo Grimond, gained three seats and won nearly twice as many votes as in 1959, partly because they had 150 more candidates.

Result:
Jeremy Thorpe (Liberal) 19,031
Basil Peto (Conservative) 13,895
Frank Paton (Labour) 4,603.
Majority: 5,136

General Election 1966. Labour's four-seat majority had been cut to just two prior to this poll. Premier Harold Wilson called an October election, hoping to capitalise on the sense of well-being in England after that part of the United Kingdom had won the football World Cup during the summer. Locally Jeremy Thorpe's majority was cut by nearly 4,000 votes as both the Conservatives, now represented by local farmer Tim Keigwin, and Labour substantially increased their share of the votes. Nationally Labour had an easy victory, resulting in a majority of 96 seats. The Liberals, still led by Jo Grimond, made a further advance, winning three more seats to take their House of Commons representation to 12.

Result:
Jeremy Thorpe (Liberal) 16,797
Tim Keigwin (Conservative) 15,631
James Rayner (Labour) 6,127
Majority: 1,166

General Election 1970. This was Jeremy Thorpe's first General Election as leader of the Liberal party. It was a bad start, as the party lost half their seats, returning to the total of six MPs that had been the case when Thorpe was first elected in 1959. In North Devon Thorpe's majority was again cut, this time to just 369 votes, only seven more than when he was first returned for the seat. This was by far the closest the Conservative, Tim Keigwin, who contested three General Elections in North Devon, came to victory. Nationally there was a surprise win for the Conservatives under Edward Heath, who gained a majority of 31. This was the first General Election in which people could vote from the age of 18, rather than the previous 21.

Result:
Jeremy Thorpe (Liberal) 18,893
Tim Keigwin (Conservative) 18,524
Chris Mullin (Labour) 5,268
Barry Gray Morris (Democratic Party) 175
Majority: 369

General Election 1974 (February). This was Jeremy Thorpe's finest hour in several respects. The North Devon electorate had been greatly increased by boundary changes which added the borough of Bideford and Bideford Rural District to the constituency. Thorpe's majority rocketed to 11,072, his highest at any of his six successful contests and, nationally, the Liberal Party he led had a net gain of eight seats, taking the party's representation in the House of Commons to 14, the highest of Jeremy Thorpe's tenure of the leadership. The two largest parties both lost a considerable share of the popular vote, largely to the Liberals, who polled two and a half times the share of the national vote that they had achieved in the previous election. With more than six million votes for the Liberals, just 14 MPs was a paltry return. Nationally Tory leader Edward Heath lost his Commons majority and attempted to win Liberal support, promising a senior Cabinet post for Jeremy Thorpe. The remaining Liberal MPs failed to support any such arrangement which, in any event, would still have left Heath short of an overall majority and dependent upon the support of volatile Northern Irish MPs. Thorpe demanded major electoral reforms in exchange for such an agreement, which was unacceptable to the Tories. When Heath finally resigned, Harold Wilson formed a minority government

Result:
Jeremy Thorpe (Liberal) 34,052
Tim Keigwin (Conservative 22,980
Terence Marston (Labour) 6,140
Majority: 11,072

General Election 1974 (October). The October 1974 general election, the second of the year and the first time that two national polls had been held in a single year since 1910, 64 years earlier, resulted in the Labour party led by Harold Wilson winning a narrow overall majority of just three seats. Jeremy Thorpe retained North Devon with a much reduced majority against a new Conservative contender and nationally the Liberals lost one seat. Subsequently Labour's majority disappeared as a result of by-election losses and defections from the party. It then required deals with the Liberals (by this time led by David Steel, after Jeremy Thorpe's resignation as leader in 1976), the Ulster Unionists and the Scottish and Welsh Nationalists.

Result:
Jeremy Thorpe (Liberal) 28,209
Tony Speller (Conservative) 21,488
Alexandra Golant (Labour) 8,536
Frank Hansford-Miller (English National) 568
Majority: 6,721

General Election 1979. When the minority Labour government finally fell, the 1979 General Election saw all three major political parties with new leaders as compared with October 1974 – Jim Callaghan (Labour), Margaret Thatcher (Conservative) and David Steel (Liberal). Jeremy Thorpe contested the election in North Devon with the shadow of his forthcoming trial hanging over his head and over his constituency party. Thorpe's October 1974 majority of more than 6,000 votes was turned into a Conservative majority of nearly 8,500. The publicity surrounding the Scott affair attracted a field in North Devon of nine candidates. Nationally Margaret Thatcher won a majority of 43 seats. David Steel's Liberals, despite adverse publicity for the party as well as for its former leader, losing just two seats to end with a Parliamentary representation of 11 MPs.

Result:
Tony Speller (Conservative) 31,811
Jeremy Thorpe (Liberal) 23,338
Antony Saltern (Labour) 7,108
Tony Whittaker (Ecology) 729
John Morley Price (National Front) 237
Frank Hansford-Miller (English National) 142
Auberon Waugh (Dog Lover's Party) 79
Henrietta Rous (Wessex Regionalist) 50
Bil Boaks (Democratic Monarchist Public Safety White Resident) 20
Majority: 8,473

Subsequent to the departure of Jeremy Thorpe from the North Devon political scene, Tony Speller for the Conservatives retained the seat in 1983 and 1987. Nick Harvey (now Sir Nick) won the constituency back for the Liberals in 1992, retaining his seat in 1997, 2001, and 2010. Conservative Peter Heaton-Jones, the MP at the time of writing, won the seat in 2015 and held it, with a reduced majority, in 2017.

Since the North Devon Parliamentary Constituency was created in 1950 there have been four Conservative MPs and two Liberal/Liberal Democrat members. However, the Liberal (Jeremy Thorpe) with 20 years and Liberal Democrat (Nick Harvey) with 23 years, have occupied the seat for 43 years of its 68 year existence.

Appendix ii
Liberal Family Dynasties

The history of the Liberal party is rich in examples of political dynasties; the Gladstones, father and sons, the Lloyd George clan, the Asquith/Bonham Carter/Grimond connections and the West Country Aclands, Foots and Lamberts.

A study of the various family connections reveals parallel lines with the history of the many and often acrimonious splits which occurred in the Liberal party over time; members of the various groups mentioned above took different stances and, in some cases, left the Liberal cause with which they had been deeply involved since their youth to support other political parties and groupings. In one or two instances the political journey was in an opposite direction, with the Liberals being the beneficiaries of a change of political heart.

During Jeremy Thorpe's lifetime his path was crossed by members of most of these groups, with the exception of the Gladstone family members, whose political careers were in an earlier era.

William Ewart Gladstone (1809-1898) began his political career as a Conservative (a High Tory in fact) and then became a Peelite, a follower of the breakaway faction of the Tory party led by Robert Peel. When the faction merged into the new Liberal party in 1859, he began the rise to power that saw him serve a total of 12 years as Prime Minister of the United Kingdom, spread over four separate terms. His political doctrine, emphasising equality of opportunity and free trade, became known as Gladstonian Liberalism. His popularity among the working classes led him to be popularly known as 'the People's William'.

His espousal of the cause of Home Rule for Ireland in 1886 led to a split in the Liberal party which helped keep it out of office, except for one brief interlude, for two decades. He left office in March 1894, aged 84, as the oldest person to serve as Prime Minister. He left Parliament in 1895 and died three years later. He was a member of Parliament for over sixty years, representing Chester, Whitby and Worcestershire East.

W. E. Gladstone's eldest son, William Henry (1840-1891) was a Liberal Member of Parliament whose accomplishments outside politics included the unlikely combination of being a noted composer of Anglican hymns and playing for Scotland in the first (unofficial) England v Scotland football international in 1870. He died in London in 1891, predeceasing his eminent father.

The youngest of the eight children of W. E. Gladstone and his wife Catherine, Herbert John (1854-1930) sat in the House of Commons as a Liberal for Leeds and later Leeds West. One at least of his political acts which was to have far-reaching consequences for British politics in the twentieth century was his 1903 conclusion of a pact with Labour leaders. This entailed agreeing that in two member constituencies, common at the time, Liberal and Labour candidates should not split the vote.

Herbert John Gladstone achieved cabinet rank as Home Secretary (1905-1910). More radical than his father, he takes credit for some of the most important social legislation ever enacted, being responsible for the Workman's Compensation Act, a Factory and Workshops Act, and in 1908 the eight hour working day underground in the Coal Mines Regulation Act. After being sacked from ministerial office in 1910 he was appointed Governor-General of the Union of South Africa (1910-1914. He was raised to the peerage as Viscount Gladstone.

The political history of the Lloyd George family – David Lloyd George, Megan Lloyd George and Gwilym Lloyd George – has been mentioned in the first chapter of this book, *Radical Politics and the West Country*.

David Lloyd George, later The Earl Lloyd-George of Dwyfor, as Prime Minister, 1914-18 war leader, and a major participant in the peace conference that followed the hostilities, campaigned under various political banners during his long and illustrious career, during which he represented Caernarvon Boroughs in the House of Commons for 55 years. From first winning the seat in 1890 (with a majority of just 18 votes) he sat as a Liberal until the General Election of 1922, which he contested as a National Liberal. At the next two General Elections, which followed closely in 1923 and 1924, he was back in the Liberal fold and continued to take the party whip until his death in March 1945, apart from a brief period around 1931 when he disagreed with the party stance on Ramsay MacDonald's National Government and described himself as an Independent Liberal.

Lloyd George, especially in his early years, rarely enjoyed a comfortable majority in Caernarvon Boroughs. The force of his personality was demonstrated when, after his death, although the Liberals retained the seat at the subsequent by-election, the party lost to a Conservative in the 1945 General Election. In 1950 the constituency was won by Labour, which held on to the seat until 1974, when it fell to Plaid Cymru.

David Lloyd George's daughter Megan, Jeremy Thorpe's Godmother, and Lloyd George's son Gwilym both started political life as Liberal MPs. Megan, as described in an earlier chapter, eventually joined the Labour party (much to the distress of Jeremy Thorpe) whilst Gwilym moved in the opposite direction, becoming a National Liberal (effectively a Tory) and serving in the 1950s Conservative governments of Winston Churchill and Anthony Eden. Home Secretary from 1954 to 1967, he refused to commute the death sentence upon Ruth Ellis, the last woman to be executed (for murder) in the United Kingdom.

The Asquith/Bonham Carter/Grimond connection had close links with the West Country and with Jeremy Thorpe personally. Herbert Asquith was Prime Minister of the UK from 1908 to 1916, when he gave way to David Lloyd George. Asquith and his first wife Helen had five children, the fourth, Violet (1887-1969) marrying Sir Maurice Bonham Carter, her father's principal private secretary, in 1915.

Violet Asquith grew up in a heavily political environment, living in 10 Downing Street at the time her father occupied it as Prime Minister, meeting and socialising with the most important figures of the day. Herbert Asquith took the nation into the 1914-18 War and from May 1915 headed a coalition with the Conservatives. From December 1916 and Asquith's resignation as Prime Minister the Liberal party was split between the followers of Lloyd George, his successor in Number 10 Downing Street, and Asquith's supporters.

For the rest of her life she was a tireless defender of her father and his reputation. Women politicians were a rare breed in the inter-war years but Lady Violet was a tireless activist for the Liberal party. She was the first woman to serve as President of the Liberal party, from 1945 to 1947. She was unsuccessful in her bid to enter the House of Commons, being defeated at Wells in 1945 and at Colne Valley in 1951. She was a close friend of Winston Churchill, himself a former Liberal Cabinet Minister and associate of her father, and he arranged for the Conservatives to stand down in Colne Valley. Lady Violet was defeated but greatly reduced the Labour majority.

Two of Sir Maurice and Lady Violet's children continued the family tradition of Liberalism Her son Mark was to secure a place in the House of Commons where his mother had failed (if only for a brief spell) whilst a daughter, Laura, married Jo Grimond, leader of the Liberals from 1956 to 1967, when he was succeeded by Jeremy Thorpe. Lady Violet was noted as a charismatic speaker, dedicated to classical Liberal politics in the same mould as her father, and she campaigned extensively, especially for her son and for Thorpe.

In 1964 she was created a life peer as Baroness Asquith of Yarnbury in the County of Wiltshire, one of the first new Liberal peers for many years and proved to be an active member of the House of Lords. Her previous title, Lady Violet, was a courtesy title from her father's elevation to the peerage as Earl of Oxford and Asquith in 1925, and her husband was a knight of the realm. She died of a heart attack, aged 81, and was buried in St Andrew's churchyard at Mells in Somerset.

Mark Bonham Carter's great achievement was to hugely boost Liberal morale in the barren 1950s by winning a by-election at Torrington.

The story of Mark Bonham Carter's successful campaign is told in Appendix 3.

The Foot family's contribution to British political history was told in Chapter 1, *Radical Politics in the West Country*, and the history of the Lambert family forms the subject of Appendix 4.

Appendix iii
Mark Bonham Carter's Torrington By-election Victory in 1958

Only those relatively few people who were politically active in the immediate aftermath of World War Two and the early years of the 1950s can really appreciate the depth of the gloom which surrounded the Liberal party at that time. The period is customarily depicted in any case, with plenty of justification, as one of austerity, rationing and grey uniformity.

Whenever the author – old enough to remember his joy at the lifting of sweet rationing – visits the Trent Bridge cricket ground in Nottingham his eye is drawn to a framed press photograph which hangs in the historic pavilion. It shows a crowd of perhaps 25,000 people watching a 1954 Ashes test against Australia, with spectators not only sitting in the stands but also occupying the grass right up to the boundary rope. It is no exaggeration to suggest that each and every spectator in the ground (and they are almost entirely male) is wearing a belted grey gabardine raincoat.

Most social commentators acknowledge that the gloom began to lift somewhat as the decade reached its mid-point, with the arrival of easier economic conditions, brighter clothes, television for the masses, rock'n'roll and Elvis Presley. Things certainly began to improve for the Liberal party and its supporters.

Mark Bonham Carter had a political pedigree. The grandson of Herbert Asquith, the last Liberal politician to command an overall majority in the House of Commons, and the son of Asquith's daughter Lady Violet Bonham Carter, a devoted defender of her father's reputation and a passionate campaigner for the Liberal cause, he was born in 1922, educated at Winchester and Balliol College, Oxford, and had what is sometimes described as 'a good war'.

Commissioned in the Grenadier Guards in 1941, captured in Tunisia in 1943, he escaped from his captors and walked 400 miles to return to the British lines.

His first venture into active politics came in the 1945 General Election when he ran second in the then Barnstaple constituency to the Conservative Christopher Peto. He renewed his acquaintance with North Devon in 1958 when the sitting MP for Torrington, George Lambert Junior, a National Liberal and Conservative member who had secured large majorities at the previous three General Elections, succeeded to a peerage on the death of his father, who had previously held the then South Molton constituency for the Liberals and the Liberal Nationals for more than 40 years. (For the full story of the Lamberts see Appendix 4.)

The constituency, founded in 1950 when the old South Molton seat was abolished and the new divisions of Torrington and Barnstaple created, consisted of the boroughs of Bideford, Great Torrington, and Okehampton, the urban districts of Crediton and Northam, and the rural Districts of Bideford, Crediton, Okehampton, and Torrington. The division was largely rural and dominated by farming, and was assumed to be an entirely safe seat for the Conservatives and their allies.

Mark Bonham Carter had different ideas, although there seemed little cause for any optimism; the Liberal Party performed poorly in 1950 when Torrington was first contested, with the victorious George Lambert Junior having a 9,000 plus majority, and the party did not even fight the seat in 1951 and 1955.

Bonham Carter made great play on the fact that geographically, North Devon was traditionally Liberal territory, whether the seat was called South Molton, Torrington, Barnstaple or North Devon. On the stump in 1958 he urged voters to recall the Liberal victories of the pre-war era, which could, he believed, be repeated.

He added: "In my visits to the various parts of the division, I have been met time and again by those who welcome the return of a strong Liberal party. This has always been a Liberal place they say and recall the great battles that were waged here and in surrounding divisions; of the giants that got returned – men like Tudor Rees, Francis Acland and many others."

When the by-election took place on March 27 1958 Bonham Carter emulated the Liberal heroes of the past by destroying the 9,312 vote majority recorded by Lambert Junior in 1955. He had squeezed home to victory by the narrow margin of 219 votes over his Conservative opponent, Anthony Royle, a London-based insurance broker who was nevertheless President of the Western Area of the Young Conservatives.

In the atmosphere of the time, the size of the majority was almost immaterial. The Liberals had won a by-election for the first time since achieving victory at Holland with Boston (Lincolnshire) in 1929. A mid-term election victory had indeed been won in Middlesbrough West in 1945 but that was mainly due to an electoral pact.

Although in 1958 the Conservative government, headed by Harold Macmillan was still reasonably popular in the country, it had suffered a blow a couple of months before the Torrington poll when all three Treasury Ministers resigned over the question of the administration's policies on economic matters. There had been slight indicators of better times for the Liberals when the party achieved second places in by elections in North Dorset in 1957 and at Rochdale earlier in 1958.

Did political commentators from the media suspect that something might be in the air in the West Country? At Rochdale earlier in the year the Manchester-based regional commercial television company, Granada, had screened the by-election. BBC Television chose the Torrington contest as only their second election broadcast since the 1955 General Election.

The media did not hesitate to point out that there was a certain irony in Bonham Carter's victory. In 1957 the Liberals had lost a seat in a contest with

David Lloyd George's daughter, Megan, who by that time had defected to Labour. Now the Liberals had gained a seat courtesy of David Lloyd George's great rival Asquith's grandson.

Conservative popularity was at a higher level by the time the next General Election was called for October 1959 with Macmillan at the height of his popularity and power. Bonham Carter was clearly going to face an uphill battle to retain the Torrington seat. He made much play while campaigning of the fact that local voters "now have the happy knowledge that they are represented by a real Liberal who is not afraid to argue with authority and who is quite free to vote according to his conscience and convictions." The comment was to some degree a jibe at the National Liberal and Conservative brand worn by George Lambert Junior at his last contest in 1955; Anthony Royle had fought the by-election as a straight Conservative.

Bonham Carter described the South West as :a part of the nation that has always reserved the right to think for themselves the home of non-conformity and the radical tradition. They struck a real blow for freedom when they returned an honest candidate fighting under true colours." His election material also contained severe criticism of the House of Commons records of South West Tory MPs. James Lindsay, soon to be defeated by Jeremy Thorpe in North Devon had, said Bonham Carter, spoken in the House on only eight occasions in nearly five years.

Mark Bonham Carter had stolen the Liberal glory in 1958 from Jeremy Thorpe, who by that time had been patiently nursing North Devon for six years and had campaigned tirelessly for his Liberal colleague at the Torrington by-election. But although Bonham Carter won the race for a place in the House of Commons, his success was short-lived. When Thorpe did eventually achieve electoral success, it was to endure for 20 years.

The 1959 General Election result was a win for a new Conservative candidate, Percy Browne, who polled 17,283 votes against 15,083 for Bonham Carter.

The Liberal contested Torrington once again in 1964, slightly denting Browne's majority. The contest was notable for the selection as Labour candidate of a name destined to become a Labour Foreign Secretary and eventually a founder of the Social Democratic party – David Owen.

Mark Bonham-Carter retired from Parliamentary politics in his own right but continued to be a trusted adviser to his brother-in-law, Jo Grimond during the Orkney and Shetland MPs tenure of the Liberal leadership. He became the first Chairman of the Race Relations Board in the period 1966–1971, and led its successor, the Community Relations Commission from 1971–1977. He was vice-chairman of the BBC from 1975–1980, but was vetoed as chairman by Margaret Thatcher. In 1986 he was created a life peer as Baron Bonham-Carter, of Yarnbury in the County of Wiltshire and he became Foreign Affairs spokesman for the Liberal Democrats. He died from a heart attack in Italy on 4 September 1994.

Both Violet and Mark Bonham Carter continued to offer support to the Liberals of North Devon; Violet contributed a message to a brochure published by the Association to celebrate its resurrection from an almost moribund state in 1951 to a flourishing organisation later in the decade.

When things went wrong for Jeremy Thorpe and the North Devon Liberals in 1979, Mark Bonham Carter recognised the hurt that would be felt by those people who had been most closely associated with the now defeated MP, for such a long time. On the day after Thorpe's shattering defeat at the General Election on 3 May of that year, he wrote to Lilian Prowse, saying: "I have often thought of you this last year and I would like to say how sorry I am that things have turned out as they have and how much I feel for you.

"I don't think there is much more to be said, but I would like you to know how much I admire and respect the work you have done and the steadfast loyalty you have shown under the most difficult circumstances that anyone could imagine."

Mark Bonham Carter

THE MAN WHO HAS SERVED YOU WELL

In the year and a half that Mark Bonham-Carter has been in the House of Commons as your representative, he has swiftly built himself a first-class Parliamentary reputation; apart from serving on several Parliamentary committees, he has also asked many pertinent questions, spoken numerous times, and answered a flood of letters from his constituents running into some thousands! In addition, he has taken the keenest interest in the local problems of the whole division. ASK ANYONE who KNOWS THE FACTS—They will confirm that BONHAM-CARTER is quite the BEST MEMBER OF PARLIAMENT THAT THIS PART OF THE WORLD HAS HAD FOR YEARS. Certainly compared with Tory members for adjoining constituencies, Bonham-Carter's record is super-human. Keep on the good work for the West—vote again for Mark Bonham-Carter.

Mark Bonham Carter's 1959 election material. *(North Devon Liberal Association Archive)*

Appendix iv
The Lamberts' Parliamentary Campaigns

The Liberal party was torn by splits in the late nineteenth and mid-twentieth centuries. The first major split came in 1886 when a faction broke away from the Liberal party, forming a political alliance with the Conservatives in opposition to Irish Home Rule. The Liberal Unionists and the Conservatives ruled in a coalition Unionist government from 1895 to 1905, retaining separate organisations until a full merger in 1912.

A signed poll card for George Lambert Senior, long-serving Liberal MP for the South Molton division, issued for the 1910 General Election. *(South Molton Museum)*

The National Liberal party (known until 1948 as the Liberal National party was a liberal political party in the United Kingdom from 1931 to 1968. The Liberal Nationals evolved as a distinctive group within the Liberal party over the issues initially arising from the official party's support for the 1929 minority Labour government led by Ramsay MacDonald and later from MacDonald's 1931 National Government. The Liberal Nationals later co-operated with and eventually merged with the Conservative party.

Lining up with the coalition under the banner Liberal National was the MP for South Molton, George Lambert, who up to that point had been faithful to the official Liberal party for 40 years. Lambert's defection to the new grouping was not unexpected; he had long been critical of David Lloyd George and was deeply opposed to the Labour party.

For 65 years from its creation in 1885 to abolition in 1950 South Molton was the twin parliamentary constituency to Barnstaple in the northern part of Devon. Both seats were abolished for the 1950 General Election and replaced by North Devon and Torrington. South Molton was a far-flung rural constituency which from 1885 to 1918 embraced the Municipal Borough of South Molton, and the Sessional Divisions of Crediton, Great Torrington, and South Molton. From 1918 until 1950 the seat took in the Boroughs of Great Torrington, Okehampton, and South Molton, the Urban District of Crediton, and the Rural Districts of Crediton, Okehampton, South Molton, and Torrington.

George Lambert was first elected for the South Molton Division at a by-election in November 1891, when he defeated a Liberal Unionist. He was subsequently returned at 10 elections (on five occasions unopposed) until being defeated in 1924 by his Unionist (Conservative) opponent. Lambert regained the seat in 1929 but that was the final occasion on which he stood as a Liberal. After his overwhelming victory as a Liberal National in 1931, with 76 per cent of the vote and a majority of more than 22,000, he held the seat comfortably in 1935. In both the 1931 and 1935 contests his only opponent was Labour, with the Conservatives/Unionists giving him a clear run.

A further General Election should have been held in 1940 but was deferred owing to the outbreak of war and the eventual creation of a coalition government under Winston Churchill. When the next General Election was called, for 5 July 1945 Lambert, by now in his late 70s, decided to step down and was succeeded by his son, George Lambert Junior, who had a comfortable majority over his Labour opponent, despite the landslide national victory for Clement Attlee's party. The Conservatives, as was the rule, did not oppose Lambert Junior, who stood, like his father in 1931 and 1935, as a Liberal National.

George Lambert Senior had been appointed to the Privy Council in 1912 and on his retirement from the House of Commons was created Viscount Lambert. He had spent 48 years and 348 days in the House, and at that time was the fifth longest-serving MP of the twentieth century.

The new seat of Torrington, created for the 1950 General Election, took in the Boroughs of Bideford, Great Torrington, and Okehampton, the Urban Districts of Crediton and Northam, and the Rural Districts of Bideford, Crediton, Okehampton, and Torrington. George Lambert Junior transferred to the Torrington constituency and won the seat with a majority of 9,539 over his Liberal and Labour opponents. Lambert Junior was again returned by the Torrington electors in 1951 and 1955, the only difference from the 1950 contest being that he stood as a National Liberal (as the grouping had by now been renamed) and Conservative.

On George Lambert Senior's death in 1958 his son inherited the title and a seat in the House of Lords. The result was a famous Liberal by-election victory, which raised the party's morale when it was at a low ebb. (See Appendix 3 Mark Bonham Carter's Torrington Victory.)

The statistical record of the General Elections contested by George Lambert Senior and George Lambert Junior between 1891 and 1955 is given below:

By-election, 13 Nov 1891: South Molton
George Lambert (Liberal) 4,222
Charles William Buller (Liberal Unionist) 3,010
Majority: 1,212

General Election 1892: South Molton
George Lambert (Liberal) 4,278
Richard Moore-Stevens (Conservative) 2,939
Majority 1,339

General Election 1895: South Molton
George Lambert (Liberal) 4,283
James J. Long (Liberal Unionist) 2,923
Majority: 1,360

General Election January 1900: South Molton
George Lambert (Liberal) Returned unopposed

General Election January 1906: South Molton
George Lambert (Liberal) Returned unopposed

General Election January 1910: South Molton
George Lambert (Liberal) 4,419
John Perowne (Liberal Unionist) 3,398
Majority: 1,021

General Election December 1910: South Molton
George Lambert (Liberal) 4,224
John Perowne (Liberal Unionist) 3,217
Majority: 1,007

General Election 1918: South Molton.
George Lambert (Liberal) 10,424.
Herbert Sparkes (Unionist - C), 8,093
Majority 2,331

General Election 1922: South Molton
George Lambert (Liberal) Returned unopposed

General Election 1923: South Molton
George Lambert (Liberal) Returned unopposed

General Election 1924:South Molton
Cedric Drewe (Unionist) 12,811
George Lambert (Liberal) 12,157
Majority 653

General Election 1929: South Molton
George Lambert (Liberal) 15,072
Cedric Drewe (Unionist) 13,567
Rudolph Putnam Messel (Labour) 2,371
Majority: 1,505

General Election 1931: South Molton
George Lambert (Liberal National) 25,700
Rudolph Putnam Messel (Labour) 3,499
Majority 22,201

General Election 1935: South Molton
George Lambert (Liberal National) 20,767
H. F. Chilcott (Labour) 5,610)
Majority 15,157

General Election 1945: South Molton
George Lambert Junior (Liberal National) 19,065
C. Lang (Labour) 9,140
Majority 9,925

George Lambert Junior and Torrington:

General Election 1950: Torrington
George Lambert Junior (National Liberal and Conservative)19,128
Elizabeth Rashleigh Liberal 9,589
Thomas B. H. Chappell 8,735
Majority 9,539

General Election 1951: Torrington
George Lambert Junior (National Liberal and Conservative) 23,162
G.R. Sargeant (Labour) 11,812
Majority 11,350

General Election 1955: Torrington
George Lambert Junior (National Liberal and Conservative) 20,124
Leonard Lamb (Labour) 10,812
Majority 9,312

Torrington by-election, 1958
Mark Bonham Carter (Liberal) 13,408
Anthony Royle (Conservative) 13,189
Leonard Lamb (Labour) 8,697
Majority 219

General Election 1959: Torrington
Percy Browne (Conservative) 17,283
Mark Bonham Carter (Liberal) 15,018
Raymond Dobson (Labour) 5,633
Majority 2,265